FROM ANKLE-DEEP:
SURVIVING CHILD SEXUAL ABUSE

*A Tell-All, Self-Help Book for Fellow Victims &
Survivors of Child Sexual Abuse (CSA)*

T0095634

SCOTT THOMAS SIEG

authorHOUSE®

AuthorHouse™
1663 Liberty Drive
Bloomington, IN 47403
www.authorhouse.com
Phone: 1-800-839-8640

Published by AuthorHouse   03/14/2013

ISBN: 978-1-4817-2969-7 (sc)
ISBN: 978-1-4817-2968-0 (e)

Library of Congress Control Number: 2013904791

<<< PREFACE >>>

*"You don't write because you want to say something;
You write because you've got something to say."*

*—F. Scott Fitzgerald (1896-1940) U.S. novelist
and short-story writer.*

Today, I take great strength in knowing that I am not alone, as I belong with an outstanding and astonishing group of 40-60 million other Americans who have been molested or abused sexually. To put that into perspective, the National Child Traumatic Stress Network reports that 'before the age of eighteen (18), one out of every four girls will be sexually abused and one out of every seven boys, too.' Recently, after my own research and trainings to be certified to help others recover and rebound from such a horrific experience, the statistics have come to life in some shape or form each working month.

The concept of writing about my experience began with a Facebook note I posted, tagging ten of my closest friends at the time, though only one no longer has a place in my life now (#Winning!). It was

Tuesday, April 5th, 2011, following another session of counseling with my doctor, midway through our eight weeks. I used an expression quite often, 'Ankle-Deep' which is more than just my book title. The label is coined comparing and identifying my previous levels of trust or commitment, as well as the status of my self-esteem and confidence that I would fully give to something or someone, including myself.

I am a survivor because I no longer feel like a victim. In fact, I never used the word victim until therapy in the spring of 2011. I have taken great strides in the last two years (2011 & 2012) to get to where I am at after a decade and a half of self-preservation; Allowing myself to have become a borderline recluse in regards to my incident for fifteen years, not only was a contrast of my personality today, but hindered my childhood and development along the way.

Prior to my attack, my family and I lived on the East Coast for some time, almost ten years. One of our frequent summer stops was driving to the Jersey shore. Yes, this was a children and family friendly destination before MTV's hostile takeover of the 'Jersey Shore' came into power. The Jersey Shore and the Atlantic Ocean beaches had a lot to offer: the light beige sand, the sounds of the waves as well as the seagulls, the shops on the boardwalk and then the ocean water itself.

My father would have a contest between us boys, before my sister was even born, to see who could find the biggest seashell in the ocean water. Even though the handicap was shared, none of us really knew how to swim. I probably had watched thirty two episodes of 'Baywatch' and still could not figure it out. Thankfully there was always a switch board operator. That would be my position on the lifeguard team by default.

In any event, because of the lack of swimming skills, I would only go into the ocean 'Ankle-Deep.' I did not trust myself, the ocean, my environment, though I did trust my panic induced parents who would scream if I went any further that I would 'die and drown' (even though the order of those two still baffles me).

Up until that point in my life, I felt like I could only go 'Ankle-Deep' in regards to my friendships, family, intimate relationships and my own self-concept and confidence. But then, I felt empowered, restored . . . almost renewed. My thoughts became clear as the text for the Facebook note just flowed effortlessly and naturally onto the screen. I bared no expense for my past as I hit reality. It was not my fault; I am not at fault. That evening in April 2011, my laptop became my vehicle of support for my reincarnated emotional health and spiritual uplifting.

At this point, that spring, I was six weeks away from moving to Los Angeles, CA. I was ready to jump into my career, start fresh and pursue a new direction for myself. Albeit, I made haste with my relocation and journey out West, but at this time, I did not settle for first available. I did not settle for 'Ankle-Deep,' as more on this analysis will be on display in my book but for now, you at least know where I am going with this.

It all came to a head, a supportive climax, if you will, at my last therapy session in Evansville, IN. That one friend out of ten who is no longer in my circle or life, however, was present for me to be a witness for my own declaration of survival from CSA. I had written a speech, a declaration of sorts for my doctor and witness, announcing my freedom, renewal and a plan to move forward. My closing was a proclamation of no longer being 'Ankle-Deep' and my new sworn strength to hold my head above ground or water (no dying and drowning here). Despite a few small snags along the way, I have honored my promises and allowances from that day and then some: hence, the charity and work I have established along the way in my own journey, as well as others.

I did not aim to have Evansville, Indiana to be the end of my therapy or counseling for myself. After all, the numbers are as gruesome as they are accurate about victims of Child Sexual Abuse (CSA). Effects include depression, guilt, shame, withdrawal from relationships, family, friends or social interaction as a whole, in addition to developing alcohol and substance abuse problems and more.

For years, I definitely fit the bill. I was depressed for years because I had carried guilt and shame with me until I moved to California. Even then, yes, I still had some days, or even at times, moments where my past haunted me, or at least the demons that came along with terrorized my psyche.

I had a difficult time growing up because of what happened to me on my eleventh birthday, being attacked and molested. It does not make it any easier when a child, such as myself, is scared and ashamed to share or open up about it, until their adult years, if even at all. According to Darkness 2 Light, another non-profit organization that rallies against CSA, 'most cases go unreported.' No child should have to experience or live through this terrifying and crippling circumstance.

Thus, this is the reason why I wrote my (first) book. Spending the majority of my life, up until this point, I hid from the truth when I was never at fault or wrong for anything. Innocence became lost but instead of regaining it, I decided if I were going to feel any blame, anger, resentment, etc. that I would transform those emotions and harbor that energy into something positive.

The book is just the beginning. I put my life, growing up as a victim and survivor of child sexual abuse, on display. It would not be fair to call it a tell-all if I did not do just that, tell it all. The appeal of me chronicling my experience is to help reach others in need, or those who know of someone in need. It may be cliché to say that if this book helps at least one person, then I have done my job. Well, this book has already helped me, so now let us see how many more souls it can heal, hearts it can repair and lives it can mend. I am a survivor of Child Sexual Abuse and here is how.

<<< CHAPTER ONE >>>

"The ultimate weakness of violence is that it is a descending spiral, begetting the very thing it seeks to destroy. Instead of diminishing evil, it multiplies it. Through violence you may murder the liar, but you cannot murder the lie, nor establish the truth. Through violence you may murder the hater, but you do not murder the hate. In fact, violence merely increases hate. So it goes. Returning violence for violence multiples violence, adding deeper darkness to a night already devoid of stars. Darkness cannot drive out darkness: only light can do that. Hate multiplies hate, violence multiplies violence and toughness multiplies toughness in a descending spiral of destruction . . . The chain reaction of evil—hate begetting hate, wars producing more wars—must be broken, or we shall be plunged into the dark abyss of annihilation."

—Martin Luther King, Jr. (1929-1968) U.S. civil rights leader and Nobel Peace Prize winner

On Thursday, August 1st, 1996, it was my eleventh birthday. We had only lived in Lombard, Illinois for two months after our family moved from the East Coast that June before. I had no friends yet, because I did not have school to meet people or find many children in my neighborhood that I felt comfortable around thus far. The neighborhood kids all did their thing and I was already a timid person even before what would happen later that evening.

Even when I lived in Pennsylvania, I had started to take Tae Kwon Do lessons through Jack & MaryBeth LaSavage. My brother, Peter, had signed up with me but quit after his first month. I almost followed suit two months later, but parents insisted on me sticking it out and did not want me to give up so abruptly seeing that I was older than he was.

So now, in a suburb adjacent to Lombard in the Chicago Land area, I had started taking lessons with another establishment. The man who ran this place was close to my age now, mid 20's. He was in his mid-twenties, tall, dark hair, athletic. He drove a nice sports car, white, if I remember correctly. My karate instructor had a nice girlfriend. To me, he had it all. He was someone I looked up to. After all, he was even friendly with our family, knowing we were new to the area. Basically, in a short period of time, my karate instructor earned a level of trust. He even had taken me home once or twice and told us places for food, gave us directions, helping us grow comfortable and at ease with our relocation.

The plan was to take a few classes, two children's classes and one adult one, all in order to gain more experience with their system and curriculum of karate to get back to the blue belt level I was at for them.

My mom had dropped me off to start the evening and the plan was to have my father pick me up. There was some disruption in the duration of my plan to say the very least.

The two children's classes went along smooth as could be. The adult class was about to begin, until upon my instructors observation, he cancelled the class. There were only two other individuals outside of me and the head instructor. Those two adults left with their belongings within two or three minutes. I was told to go ahead and wait for my dad to pick me up when the class would originally leave. I was welcomed to stay behind and he would keep me company.

I will not hesitate to share this observation of my own, as it never struck my mind until typing the prior paragraph. I was never offered to call my mom or dad to tell them about this development. He just told me to sit down in the office and to hang out there. He closed the door behind him. I was distracted by the pictures of him he had on his wall with different celebrities like Chuck Norris and 'Bozo the Clown.' Yes, people . . . in 1996 these two were celebrities.

Before I had looked aside from the pictures and back at him, he began to tie my hands down to the chair at the wrist. My right hand first, then my left. Then, stepped behind me, over my right shoulder and started to massage both of my shoulders for about a good minute or so. He said nothing, which made for an awkward silence.

He had reached for a bottle from his cabinet behind his office desk. The cap was removed and placed on his desk. Walking over with the bottle, my instructor had walked over to me and began to pour the liquid past my lips and into my mouth. I had a choking, gaging response to it as I identified it as a form of booze or hard liquor right away. By comparison from sipping on my parents' drinks a few times following this incident, when they were not looking, my best hypothesis is that the liquor was vodka.

The next twenty minutes or so changed my life forever. I was sexually molested by my karate instructor in a grotesque and perverse manner. I was forced-fed liquor, taken advantage of and became a victim of Child Sexual Abuse that night, on my eleventh birthday. The details of my attack were so vivid and terrorizing that it would eventually reside in my nightmares, on and off for years. Even today, but in a more off-set, unrealistic way.

I was in tears, but not yet crying. My eyes were filled up with moisture so quick, but my cheeks still felt dry. Not a tear ran down my face yet. Then, I remember using my sleeve to wipe my face, following a sniffle and the first couple of tears. After he left the bathroom, he yelled back at me to get ready before my dad gets here. I looked at the clock and my dad was not there yet, as it was six minutes until 8 p.m.

I quickly gathered my uniform into my bag after changing into another t-shirt and gym shorts. The instructor came over to me and placed his hands on my shoulders, no longer massaging but squeezing as if he needed to exert anymore force or control over me. The words he uttered were 'I know where you live and if you tell anyone, I will find out.'

From that night on and many nights after that, for years, I kept tight lipped about that evening, about the whole experience. Even when my father picked me up and saw my eyes were a little red and I had my hands shaking the slightest but noticeable to him. He asked if I had a good time. I did not cry, but I screamed back at him and said 'I hate this place. I don't want to come back!'

I remember coming home and rushing straight to my bedroom. I skipped dinner and snack, preoccupied with burying my disturbed face into the pillow. I would fall asleep not long afterwards. That was the last time I ever set foot in that establishment. The last few weeks of summer dragged on, as I had very little interaction with anyone outside of my family. If I had a friend to hang out with, maybe things would have turned out different, perhaps better for me.

In addition to now being an introvert as well as both mentally/emotionally distressed, I had to begin the 6th grade, a.k.a. middle school, with a whole new group of peers, three states and a time zone away from anyone I had already been familiar with.

My new academic foundation for the next 3 years was Glen Westlake Middle School, home of the Wildcats. My teachers were Mr. Grumbles and Mrs. Bucholz. Mr Grumbles taught Math, Science and Social Studies,

Mrs. Bucholz taught English and Reading/Literature, but also had another Social Studies class.

I had an accent that my classmates picked up on, being from the East Coast. The Pennsylvania heritage I developed I guess merited a nickname, Quaker Oats. Cute, could have been worse, . . . oh but give it time. I am all about ownership and I was a nerd in middle school. At Glen Westlake, I was an honor student, on Student Council, a member of the Environmental Club and I even tried the Drama Club but I figured after my summer, drama was the last thing I needed. Though, my membership to both has panned out since I sometimes come across to have a lot of drama in my environment.

My friends were lacking, as the only people I really began to know where to the left and right of my locker (Justin R. had his locker next to me—we still talk even today), as well as a girl named Bailey. She had also attended the same karate place as me, but I never shared with her what happened, until now I suppose, if she's reading this book.

My parents were also animate on me being more social. They tried to corral me to do things outside of school with my peers. To be honest, I only made the excuse I liked studying and doing after school clubs more, instead of being forward about why with my parents. I was nervous to make friends, have people judge me or tease me because of another man molesting me. It was kind of gross to kids, never really talked about in schools. D.A.R.E would come to our school, promoting drug awareness and prevention. But I never remember anything about Child Sexual Abuse awareness or prevention. At this point, my parents still did not know, nor did anyone else, except for the attacker and well, God.

About this time, I received the first of quite a few letters and cards in the mail with a 'Special Offer' to come back to that karate place where I was attacked. Thankfully, my mom laughed at it and tore it up before disposing of it. Such direct marketing tactics were just that: a means of luring me back for perhaps round two, a repeat performance of my eleventh birthday.

My grades and extra-curricular activities were my main focus for the first six weeks or so until my parents approached me about karate again. Despite the investment in my karate lessons for the past three and half years before my attack, my mom and I drove around other neighboring suburbs of Lombard for alternate karate schools. It took a couple places and some evening journeys, but one stuck out and caught my interest and attention right away.

The U.S. Martial Arts Academy in Glen Ellyn, Illinois became my new home for martial arts. I emphasize the term 'home' here because it would eventually turn out to be just that. Grand Master Don Jing Kim and his lovely family, wife and two children, ran this establishment off Roosevelt Road. I would spend a glorious and most eventful seven years with this school. Credit is due as many of my skills I have developed and adapted are because of the life lessons I learned from their curriculum. I hope that even still today they do as it has been a year now since I have visited.

From that October in 1996 onward, I would take lessons and meet people my age. Though, the level of social interaction my parents were wanting out of me was not met, they were satisfied by my accomplishments there.

I met a few people in my classes, a handful of boys and girls each, that I would talk to and converse with. However, I never really found that partner in crime or companion, until Halloween. This particular 'friend to be' would actual be an object as oppose to a person. My bedroom was downstairs in our house in Lombard and my parents, brothers' and sister's bedroom would be upstairs. Freedom in the nocturnal hours was received and

There were people who talked about it at my bus stop, mainly eighth graders. I decided to take the initiative and to try drinking beer at the age of 11 on Halloween, while watching TV in my room that night. That Thursday evening, I took four beers, thinking, actually more so, guessing at what it would take to 'get drunk.' I knew beer was softer in terms of liquor than vodka or anything of that nature, like what was used in my attack.

Most children who stay up watching horror movies on network or cable programming go to bed or wake up in their sleep with nightmares from such instilled viewings. In addition to the beer, about three and a half cans worth in, my night terrors began of me being molested. I got myself worked up over what happened on my birthday just three months ago from Halloween. I grew restless and struggled to sleep.

I would have flashes of the attack that lasted three or four seconds as it played out in my mind agin, lapsing in my daydreams and nightmares as if it were a broken movie reel, skipping to the highlights, or in this case lowlights of this incident. Looking at the third or fourth marketing postcard for the first karate place did not make for a great day either. I thought I was over that place, as well as what had happened. Guess not!

There is one memory of where I almost told my father what happened. He and I set out on a jog, run of sorts. We journeyed the bike path from Lombard to Elmhurst and made it from our house to my grandmothers. This is the sort of thing we used to do, some small racing contests or a competition of 'h-o-r-s-e' or 'Around the World' or even tennis. My dad would win, never letting up. I respected that, but my competitiveness hated it.

There I was for at least a couple of hours, just jogging away with my father with no one else around to hear or see us talk about it. But yet, I could not zero in on how to present to him his son was molested a few months ago. There aren't any icebreakers or seg-ways I can think of to lead into that one. So, again, the subject was swept under the carpet.

The holidays shortly loomed around. I was slightly closer to getting my black belt, well on my way to Honor Roll at Glen Westlake Middle School, but nowhere near having a healthy social life with my peers. My friends on Friday nights became the ladies and gentlemen of Roller Derby from World Skating League that played on the Nashville Network (now Spike TV) and Bud Light.

My Saturdays would be full of karate, too, as every first Saturday of the even months would be our belt promotion testing. December was my first test. I remember my mom filling out the form and review of how the student, referring to me, was doing at home. Chores, trustworthiness, respect and more were all categories emphasized on the evaluations to being a good student in and out of the 'do jang' as they call the school or area for learning Tae Kwon Do in Korean.

Yes, looking back on it, I was not the best son. I would lie and fib a couple of times to get out of trouble. By a couple I mean I lost count after 50,043. The biggest lie I was telling was the one truth I was hiding. I do not know if it would have made a difference back then on my down days when I was upset or sad looking back at it. However, I could guarantee you, on a good day like today, it could have possibly prevented some collateral damage in the years to follow.

I remember one Christmas present in particular was my first weight bench. My gosh I was made fun of for admitting that I got one of those things because I did not appear to be the kind of kid to want, use or have any clue of what one of those looked like. A boxed set of World Book Encyclopedia, a pocket protector or a gift card to Barnes & Noble was more believable.

I used it every so often. I was skinny at first, having body issues and developing the precursor for acute body dysmorphia. I feel like I more or less was picking at myself because I did not know how to love myself, thin or thick. This reoccurring theme in my life would finally come to ahead in college, but we shall stick with the chronological presentation of my 'Facts of Life.'

My diet was poor. I would not eat a lot in front of people, especially at school. My real intake of calories would be done in secrecy, often in my room. Thus, binge eating developed. Calories became friends and in secrecy and in bulk, too. I would store and leave food in my room all the time as if I had pantries in my closet, desk, bed and stored in toys. Yes, at the age of 11 and 12, I still played with my G.I. Joe's. This was even before Channing Tatum had anything to do with the franchise or movie. Perhaps, though, it is still kind of lame . . . but not any more lame than 'Pogs' or X-men would have been. Damn, I had both of those, too.

Anyways, slowly, I saw a gut on me. I was not happy with the way I looked in the mirror. The same perspective came with my face, too, as I was I felt fat and ugly before the end of the school year. Good grades, a couple more belt ranks closer to my black belt with the same quantity of friends was pretty much my theme the second half of 6th grade for me.

Then, the summer came. Most kids my age do big things, socialize with friends, go to birthday parties, and play baseball. Nope, I read, studied. I even buried my eyes into a dictionary. Before the first month of summer was over, I upgraded to a thesaurus. I was too ashamed of what happened and myself to want to play, or do anything with children my own age, guy or girl.

That summer, in June, I did test for what they called 'Bo-Black Belt' which was the belt before my Black Belt. The requirement was you were highly recommended to wait six months after receiving this rank to go for Black Belt. My mom had given me a one-on-one on at her work, a restaurant off North Avenue in called Crossroads (There is some irony in that name). It was about being a better son and listening, cutting down on my back talk and other recommendations that I clearly have followed now in the year 2012. So in August, the same week of my birthday, I tested for my black belt.

I was not a bad kid, like the ones you see being sent off to military school on Maury or back in the day it was also Sally Jesse Raphael. On a random note, my favorite was Jenny Jones, she was the greatest. I think I had a crush on her. Add that to the list with Vanna White and Heather Locklear on early childhood crushes.

My birthday was approaching, August 1st that summer. Nothing really built up in my head in terms of dwelling on the events, at least not above the normal amount of spontaneous flashbacks. I do remember my cake and blowing out the candles. The mail came in and cards poured in from family. One postcard was another marketing letter from the original karate place I attended.

I was just ready to go back to school. My teachers, text books and homework were my friends. They kept me out of trouble and helped prevent any of my negative thoughts or flashbacks from what happened develop in my head, for the most part.

I remember seventh grade was packed with events. I had the reputation of being a smart kid. Some of my peers would get excited to get a better score than me on a test than I did. To be honest, some of those people probably could not verify that memory, but when you hold onto so much in your life, you retain a deep memory back. Sometimes, I swear I am a mutant with telepathy, minus the baldness and mobile chair (Yet another childhood character reference).

That year, I took an active part of our Character Counts Program at our school and made extra efforts in extra-curricular activities. We got vouchers for good deeds, complimented and praised for kindness and going above expectations in the classroom and during lunch.

I took a liking to dancing for some reason, too. The music I listened to would be the hits of the week on B96 in Chicago on the weekends and I remember dancing like a fool in my room. My door would be closed. I would be wearing my blue jeans, an oxford, tennis shoes and my goofy orange-colored blazer. That is correct, I was channeling my 'Motown Philly' ensemble, courtesy of Boyz II Men music video . . . ABC, BBD!

It became a release for me. If I had a flash back of my attack, which every year, more would occur, I would dance. Choreography, freestyle . . . I do not know if I was good at the time since my only audience was Heaven or any outside birds or insects who would creep a peek into my window. But, Lord I would dance until I sweat through my little Hanes t-shirts and briefs. I admit it, I rarely wore boxers until the middle of seventh or eighth grade. I was that kid, in addition to my high aptitude with my social life and other things cool. The type of underwear determines the type of man.

There was one group of friends I always talked with, socialized and clicked with really well. Seven in total: the girls were Samantha S., Megan S. and Lauren K.. The dudes were James L. & James P. and Larnell L.. We had the same homeroom with Mrs. Brunell. Silent ball and McDonald's parties was our moniker. The 'Arch Deluxe' was my go-to culinary sin. Now extinct, that was my default order. Sometimes, it would be like a Sam's Club order and I would go in bulk, two or three per occasion. Food was rarely my comfort, but I was comfortable eating in front of others in middle school, as that would change in years to come.

I added to my extra-curricular activities with Newspaper Club. Seventh and eighth graders wrote for the school newspaper. I wanted to be a journalist or a detective, something of that nature. I came close as I went to college for advertising and public relations. I blame the combination of X-Files and detective shows I would watch on Friday night Fox television. It is funny how television often dictates or encourages certain career choices. If I could swim I would be a lifeguard because of Baywatch, but as previously mentioned, I could only be a switchboard operator because of the 'Ankle-Deep' thing.

There was one act of confidence I exhibited in asking a girl to the dance with me. I was still on Student Council and helped plan and set up the school dance that quarter. The girl was Jennifer and she was even an 8th grader. Even though it was just a year in difference, it still scored points with my peers. Plus, it gave me a chance to show off those moves my TRL mimicking days taught me.

I had fun and I believe she did, too. We were just friends, but that did not matter. I put myself out there to be rejected and I was not. I got to share the company of someone I went to school with, yes at school still, but not during a group project or lunch. It was one of my few social interactions with my peers that children tentatively are supposed to experience.

A month or two later, I invited Samantha to come see me receive my Black belt. My grandmother, her second husband, Carl was there, along with both of my parents. This day was one of the few with innocence that I had as a child. Something so proud was just as pure. Much is the same with my very success today at the age of 27.

After my reception for my Black Belt, we all went to the mall, Yorktown Mall. My parents gave me a $20 bill for Sam and I. I suppose it was our first 'date':

The type that the guy buys the meal at the Food Court for both the girl and himself. Apparently, the protocol for such was never forwarded to me in an e-mail or text message. I spent the majority of it on basketball trading cards and she was stunned how fast I made that transaction.

Note to current pre-teens . . . never spend your parents money designated to treat you and your lady towards a material purchase in the manner that I did. My grandmother, the straight-shooting, honest, classy matriarch of our family she is, made damn sure to tell me I f*cked up without using such a decorative adjective.

In the spring of my 7th grade, I posted my highest GPA's: a 3.7 and a 3.4, respectively. These were the highest Honor Roll marks of my life, I believe. Warning signs of someone who is depressed, suicidal and with a low self-esteem do not traditionally merit those marks. The opposite tends to occur. The semester I was most miserable was when I performed the best in school.

One day in seventh grade, I remember some older kid put a 'Kick Me' sign on my back (The only one of my life at the point, surprisingly). My math teacher, Mr. Surdam, caught on to what was going on . . . some peer hazing that needed an intervention. I was in tears, returning to the classroom before our chapter test. I had the runny nose and eyes, sniffles and shaky hands to compliment my raffled posture.

I remember being in the seat and the students around me took notice. They asked me if I was okay. I could not tell them the truth because I did not want to feel weak. So, I proceeded as if nothing was wrong. One girl, Stefanie B. had always joked about cheating on homework or silly antidotes like that. She had yelled to me, 'Scott, can I ask you a question?' My response was as follows: 'Yes, Stefanie, I know to move my arm so you can see my answers to the test.'

Mr. Surdam was shocked because I think he thought I was half serious, but more so relieved I appeared to be in better spirits. This is the first memory I have of using humor to mask my true feelings, hardships and pain.

The conclusion to my seventh grade was not as masked as that joke. One day, I believe the Friday before the last weekend of seventh grade, I went to my locker and two of my friends asked me what was wrong. It was Samantha and Megan from my homeroom. I was flat out honest and direct, sharing that I hated my life and I had enough, more or less. I told them I was going to kill myself that weekend.

Within minutes, they told our counselor, Mrs. Thompson. She came to find me during my last class of the day, Art. I remember having people in that class I was starting to be friends with: Madi M., Lauren P., Brandon S. and others. She mentioned we had something to talk about when we got down to her office but I already knew what the topic of discussion was before her series of friendly, genuine but probing questions began.

We got to her office that Friday afternoon. She had asked the most generic question at that point 'what was going on?' My response of 'I am not happy' was accompanied with tears and sobs, shaky hands and trembling. I struggled to put sentences together. I was preparing to be honest. I could not muster the strength to share that I was molested. I was in too much fear of what I shared with my friends just thirty minutes ago. I chalked it up, almost over dramatizing the hazing, the teasing and the feeling of being a social outcast. Half of which was my doing, I acknowledged. But at the age of twelve, who takes on that level of ownership and guilt. One who is probably scarred and plagued with demons from something so tragic and dark like the events of my eleventh birthday.

I admitted to announcing I was going to kill myself and that I had a lot going on. People say 'what is going on with an adolescent that makes them want to take their own life.' I was living proof of that perspective. What I was holding onto was so deep and heavy, living had seemed so expendable.

So, Mrs. Thompson's questions began to probe even more into every aspect and at the layers, except for me being molested. I shared I felt like I did not have many friends; I shared I did not like how things were with my parents; I shared thoughts and feelings about my looks and how I did not feel loved. It nearly brought my own counselor to tears to see an honor roll student who was so involved with student counsel and more, be so happy and energetic on the outside, but to hold onto so much pain and resentment for one's self. She was clearly struck with shock and bewilderment from this anomaly.

There was a pen and paper out in front of her. Using my honesty as a craft to establish the first steps towards recovery, she had asked me to sign the paper, saying that I promised not to cause bodily harm or to hurt myself over the weekend and that I would safely return to school on Monday. I complied and put my signature on the appropriate make-shift contract.

My father received a phone call. He handled it quite aggressively. He conveyed emotions of disappointment, sadness and a slight trace of anger, as if I had broken something in the house or stole from the mall. My mom came home from work and tried to play the sensitive card the next day to counter balance. Speaking of balance, there was none. I think both of my parents were just shocked. Counseling was the next step and during the summer, I spent my time speaking to a therapist, sometimes with my mom in the room.

Megan and Samantha that Monday felt so bad, but for what I do not know. I did not have any anger or angst towards them. They apologized for what they did, though, they quite possibly saved my life because you know never know how serious one could be when they so casually announce they have had enough and are ready to check out of life, especially at such a young age. To this day, I could not tell you if I would have fallen through. Perhaps not that weekend, but if those words came out of my mouth to friends, I firmly believe that I may have eventually made good on them if Samantha and Megan did not go seek the help and aide of Mrs. Thompson.

The summer was filled with more karate and now the doctor's appointments. We kept it a secret between my parents and myself only. My brothers and sister did not know what was going on at the time. They did not really need to know since they all were ten years old, or younger than that even.

I remember the office was off North Avenue by mom's work, a restaurant named Crossroads. Hence, why I told you the name of the restaurant was ironic: Crossroads. The goal of therapy was to become and feel more comfortable with myself and around others my age. A lack of social activity was diagnosed to be a part of the problem. I believed it. I went along with it all because it helped cover the truth: that I was molested as a kid. I can't believe that I averted another opportunity where I was safe and surrounded by the appropriate personnel, but I did. Consistency developed a life-cycle of covering the truth about my past and how I was both scared and scarred.

The results had not changed any; I still had only associated with children my age from karate. I did not know people's phone numbers from class or anything of their contact information, besides the handful I already had. So therapy ended at the end of summer and my parents just did the best they could. I do not blame them for the things that happened. Back then, I may have thought that at times, but certainly acted out as such. However, at the modest adult age, in my mid-20's, I do not today.

Today, I think about how hard it would be to learn and discover such an incident about my own children (if I were to have any that is . . . and yes, my plans are to have some soon some day). Being the parent of a child who is willing to take their own life would be difficult, so I always gave my parents the best I could in terms of emotional allowances for going through that.

There was not much to my birthday, although that summer was our first to the Wisconsin Dells. It was a frequent summer destination for us, as it took the place of the Jersey Shore beach trips. Staying in character, I avoided the water. I still wore a swim suit which was a two piece (trunks and a white—T), as I had not felt comfortable with my shirt off. I would get damp because I would only go 'Ankle-Deep' but I prevented myself from going all in: Story of my life. I think this is why I could never gamble. I have no interest. I try to play my life safe and mundane. Well, the mundane part would shortly change once I hit college, as you will soon learn.

Eighth grade crept around: Another series of new classes, classmates, teachers and avoiding socializing. Although, it did get better for me. The first day of eighth grade, it was homeroom in Mrs. Brunell's class (again). Justin C. walked in and said, 'Scott Sieg is in this class, saweet!' That made my day right there and quite possibly, my whole first quarter. Instantly though, I turned it around in my head secretly thinking he said that because he knew about last year and how I spent my summer speaking to a therapist after my suicidal comments. I had no reason to question his authenticity in his remark. It just became second nature to doubt anything about me was in fact 'saweet.'

I was still heavily involved with karate and not with my social life with my friends. Flashbacks became more reoccurring, rarely in the day though. They were basically only at night in my sleep. I think having a bedroom downstairs to myself helped to make my situation develop more. The isolation that created added to my dynamic growing up. I felt independent but it was not necessarily by training and development but more so by circumstances and environment. The separate bedroom on a my own floor was symbolic.

I was too young to get a hold of drugs, it was not around me. I paid attention in my third year of our school doing D.A.R.E. In taking notes, a way to get high and fuzzy was aerosol. I would sniff and inhale white out, Sharpies, rubber cement, markers, spray paint. I was the junkie who was a visit down Aisle 7 at Menards or Home Depot away from a binge or relapse.

It was a short lived, but it was still a serious offense to my body in addition to the effects of drinking beer at such a young age. Feeling out of sorts and not proper did help with the pain, at least in the sense of a quick fix. That is all aerosol was to me for those few months, a quick fix. The beer was a longer, more sustainable means of coping.

The holidays approached and shortly after Thanksgiving, I got sick. I swear that like I had bronchitis, pneumonia and probably mono all back to back. For a kid who felt like they were battling weight issues because of puberty and emotional eating, this was the best Christmas present. I lost a significant amount of weight. I barely ate, was often sweating in bed and throwing up. Stomach flu became a quality abdominal workout for me during this time. Bicep curls were mimicked in the form of lifting the toilet seat up and down.

I came back after about a five week break (counting the time off for Winter Break) because of my collection of illnesses as people were talking. Some thought I moved, some thought I was hospitalized, as they noticed my new shape and body composition. They were shocked as I just rolled with it. That is how I usually am. I may want something so bad, like a new look, or a new material object or even something that is intangible.

Nevertheless, once I get it, I just go with it. I appreciate it, but I am never really 'happy' about it. Some things I am, but usually, I am just even-keel and very tranquil about that kind of stuff. It is like pretending that being content is happy, but when you are not happy, contention is boring. Some may call that just being a high maintenance, royal pain in the *ss.

Now, the new skinny Scott did have some progress that he made. I approached a teacher, my science and social studies teacher. I told her that I had a friend who was bothered by a man, I did not use the word molested but I began a trend of using certain words that were synonyms for words to see if she could decipher my cryptic message. I think it worked but the situation was still very secretive and came off as generic research more than self-application.

I told her that there were multiple letters in the mail and there was an encounter sexually. She told me that she highly recommends to have my friend tell his parents, a counselor and to get more people involved. I saw how serious and almost aggressive in her response for my 'friend's' well-being and I took her advice to heart.

I decided on the bus ride home from school that I was going to tell my parents what had happened to me on my eleventh birthday. My thought was that I was better off telling my mother and my father. I grew tired of the flashbacks, the sheltering of my life and no longer wanted to feel so detached from my own childhood. I victimized myself more than anything after the events that took place in August 1996.

After the last few years, though, recently, I find out that is what victims and survivors do. They develop that pattern or habit of victimizing and receive it from peers because it becomes a cycle for us. We feel ashamed and guilty at first or shortly after being molested. Others around us may contribute to those emotions or stances by telling us we deserve it, or we asked for it, etc. That is not the case, but quite easy to fall, well . . . victim to believing in, even in our adult years.

That day in February 1999, I felt ready to break the cycle. My parents had a bombshell to almost trump mine, though. They shared with me that we would be moving over Spring Break to Naperville, another suburb of Chicago. I shifted focus and changed gears. I instantly turned this into a belief of having safety and recovery in my head. As if moving was therapy or treatment itself, I never told my parents anything I was planning on.

In fact, I half way pretended I was upset about another relocation. Once I heard my mom say I could stick with the same karate school, the U.S. Martial Arts Academy, I was okay with it. I was not enthusiastic about it in front of her, but I rolled with it. Again, there was a lack of expressing happiness. I quickly developed this belief that if I was away from where it happened, what happened to me in terms of growing up would change, ultimately leading to me feeling like it never happened. It was not so much about forgetting about being molested, just wanting to eliminate the feeling, cognitions, terrors and more that plagued me in the aftermath.

So, I went in to school telling people the news. Much to my surprise, my peers were disappointed and saddened. They genuinely conveyed to me that they would miss me. The next month, my last at Glen Westlake was spent finding out how much people gave a damn and cared about me. I found out I was one of the nicest, sweetest and funniest people they knew. Who would have thought?! My classmates thought so highly of me; they shared the same view on me as my teachers did, of me being the loyal, kind and fun kid who moved from the East Coast more than two years previous.

My last week was full of activity. It was all mainly during school hours. That Monday, I was told to go to the office and pick up the mail. I took advantage of my good student, trustworthy-natured reputation and paraded around the school visiting past teachers to share the news that I would be moving. Of course, I did not get in trouble, even when I told Mrs. Brunell the truth about what I was doing along with getting the mail.

In the middle of that week, I went to orientation for my new middle school. It would be home for me just for the fourth quarter, but I was ready for a chance to start over and make new friends instead of just being friendly with classmates. Coincidentally, my assistant principal, Mr. Anderson was previously employed at my new middle school, Gordon Gregory Middle School. He knew two of my future teachers on my new schedule that they had given me. I showed it to him when I came back to homeroom late, the day of my new school orientation.

That Friday, a couple of students and myself were told to wait next door in the other classroom as other students were bringing in their projects from the advanced science class . . . or so I was told and made to believe this was the case. In just a few short hours, I would be 'victim' to something positive in my life, for once. Mr. Anderson & Mrs. Brunell, Mrs. Homeir and my classmates had planned a Surprise Going-Away Party for me. It was incredible! Of course, with my dumb found luck, I ended up getting laughed at because

Sprite came out my nose when I was laughing about something stupid I said. That feeling stings when it happens: liquid protruding from your nostrils. If that is my only embarrassing moment from such a party, I will take it.

> *"He who receives a benefit with gratitude repays the first installment on his debt."*

> *—Lucius Annaeus Seneca (4 B.C.-65 A.D.) Roman philosopher, statesman and dramatist.*

This was one of the nicest gestures ever but it made me regret not going further into becoming better friends outside of school and taking chances on being closer with more people. Like the type of active friends that would go to the mall together or catch a movie or watch a Sunday football game together on TV.

Now, returning home, my parents asked me how my last day was. I told them about the party and that it was nice. I left it at that. For once, I felt happy and did not just roll with it. I embraced it for the moment that it was. I felt good about myself, all things considering. Moving to Naperville may have been exactly what the doctor or therapist prescribed. But having an 'out of mind, out of sight' approach to my healing and dealing with being molested almost three years later was negligent of what issues I had developed.

I think this is the first of my many coping mechanisms in terms of avoidance. I say that because my problems and struggles would only continue and build up steam in my new school and new environment. Naperville would become the next stage to some of the deepest, closest and evolving moments in my growth and some of my emotional demise, to date.

<<< CHAPTER TWO >>>

MOVE TO NAPERVILLE

*"We cannot always build the future for our youth,
but we can build our youth for the future."*

*—Franklin D. Roosevelt (1882-1945)
former U.S. president*

I swear I moved to the Beverly Hills of the Midwest. Naperville was full of big houses, fancier cars, better looking people, etc. Everything about it just screamed bigger and better. So naturally, fitting in was already hard for me since whatever new-found confidence I gained from my last day at Glen Westlake got lost with the move to Gordon Gregory.

My 'buddy,' as Gregory Gordon Middle School called new student guides, was Jeff B. He was my guide for school. We had a lot of the same classes. I met so many people in the first day: Lauren C. and Scott D., Joe M., Lindsay V., Kristen P. and Nina D., Ben B. & Ben R. Luckily, I had a real good memory so keeping track of the new names and faces came easy. The deeper talking and getting to know them part was something I was struggling to do naturally over the years.

Humor usually breaks the ice, or so the say. I truly feel this is where my attempts to be clever, witty and funny started to form out of habit or develop within my own personality. The origin of my wise-crack coping mechanisms formulated from just trying to start a conversation or feel more comfortable in a brand new school.

The girls were so pretty, not to say the girls from Lombard were not, because they both were. But the girls in Naperville had looked like they were Xeroxed from a magazine or imported from a runway to the school hallway.

I was still the tall, skinny, borderline scrawny, frail looking nice guy, but extremely shy now. My voice did not get the same rewards of puberty that my height and leg hair did. Bummer! That is still sort of the same deal today, minus the leg hair. Double bummer!

The one class I looked forward to the most was P.E. Volleyball was the sport of the quarter or series and it was one of my best. I would dive for the ball and could serve it well. Other than my jokes, I felt like this was about all I had to offer to make friends: One-liners and good volleyball playing skills. To think I was not made the Spring Fling King that first week is a total sham . . . Sarcasm!

There was not a lot to that fourth quarter in eighth grade at Gregory, though. Even graduation was more like attending a funeral for an unknown person. I walked around, some faces looked familiar but I did not put effort in to really bonding with anyone. I had met people, they were friendly. But again, that 'Ankle-Deep' thing kept limiting me and holding me back from what I wanted.

Actually, graduation was actually embarrassing for me. That Sunday beforehand, I attended a White Sox game with my dad and brother, Pete, spending almost the full day in the sun. It was the day before our class trip to Bicentennial Beach and I was burnt. I mean I am talking orange, blistered and irritable. I wore my graduation gown with oversized boots and just a pair of underwear beneath the gown just because of the pain on my skin.

I tried using that as an excuse not to go, but my parents still forced me. It was their moment as well, I guess. Although, I would have rather graduated with my peers from Glen Westlake because they felt more like friends, not a knock on the people from Naperville. I just call a spade, a spade. But I was a red spade, who suffered from too much sun during those 48 hours.

Another summer went on without any excitement; another dry vacation to the Wisconsin Dells for me and another 'No Peers in Sight' birthday celebration. I should not use the word 'dry' because now that my own room was at the beginning of the stairs and still away from my parents' room, I would still sneak a few beers and drink in my room.

I never got smashed or hammered in my room. Just tipsy trying to keep myself entertained. You could be bored with nothing to do and it sucks. However, if you are bored with nothing to do and you have a beer in your hand, it looks better and somehow is more entertaining. Your outlook on the situation somehow, magically improves. Television shows became funnier, music became cooler to listen to. Hell, even my dance moves to TRL became better, so I thought. Yep, those are the effects of drinking and I learned that by age 14.

Yeah, that summer was uneventful. Then, abruptly, came freshman year at Neuqua Valley High School. Still in Naperville, this school was huge, harboring the other middle school graduates from Gregory and a second middle school, called Crone Middle School. It felt as if I was relearning new names and faces all over again with some extra ones, too.

First period was World History with Mrs. Bushell, I believe. Again, I have a ridiculously intense memory for details and facts (so I hope this one is right). I retain information and memories very well. I could tell you almost all of my teachers and classes, at least 90% accurately.

I had a crush on this girl named Caroline. She was cute and blonde. Still is. I was attracted to her contagious smile, beautiful eyes and she laughed at my jokes. Or she at least laughed at me, whatever. Caroline still was the highlight of my morning, or school day for that matter.

It came time around the Holidays when I asked her about going out. I was rejected. But, it did not affect our friendship. Caroline was a genuine person and the type of girl who wished well, even though you knew she was well on her way. Her sister Emily was the same way; we would later become acquaintances, too.

In any event, I still was not making a whole lot of friends. To my perspective, I was only friendly with my peers, coming across to them as funny and up-beat. Mainly, I thought people just viewed me as being average, or normal. Do not judge a book by its cover, though . . . much less your own.

I was not normal. I drank in my bedroom alone at an early age because I had built up such a high level of shame and guilt in my life after what happened on my 11th birthday. I could not shake the demons as they grew larger and deeper. I would muff my face into a pillow many times and many nights, wanting to be someone else, wanting to be someone different from who I was then. There were moments where I would hope I did not wake up in the morning. The few prayers I would ever form would be with my demise in mind.

Each morning that I did wake up, I dreaded it for the longest time. I would feel miserable, lonely and disgusting: both on the outside and in. Nonetheless, I knew people did not look at me this way, so I trudged forward in putting my efforts into being a positive, happy and friendly person. Perhaps the friendly part was not a struggle, but the other two were. I knew in the back of my mind, something had to give before I would break.

There was one moment I did open about myself. I felt embarrassed about anything about me because I was so embarrassed about being molested as a child. I use the term child, but it was just a few years back at this time, so I was still technically a child then, too. Being jettisoned to another new school, carrying such a burden and trying to fit in felt like a punishment. English class with Mr. Meyer was the outlet of a little sharing about myself. I took a gamble and shared with my classmates about my martial arts background as part of a project. Although, I figured I would leave the part out about the whole Child Sexual Abuse thing. I think the visual aide requirement may make people uncomfortable if I went that route. After all, I had been used to not talking about it. So why break the cycle now?! I should have, but not in this particular outlet.

It impressed some people that I was a black belt in Tae Kwon Do. It was nothing to be embarrassed about. When you assume the worst, you get just that. Just stepping outside my comfort zone, I knew people felt like they had a connection, or something to talk about with me. The situation was vice-versa now, too.

There is something I took from Mr. Meyer and his class that I always remember. He would tell his students to be positive and focus on the good in life. You can't go through life or the hallways of Neuqua with your head down. Chin up, look forward and just walk. It is true. I do not know if he was referring to me or it was an ambiguous situation, but I knew I fit the bill. Deep down inside I did not want to be the kid who had focused on the negative, let alone lie to his peers and classmates about being happy just to keep people at bay. But it was surely a work in progress to change that mindset and some personality traits.

The same semester had another silver lining that ranked above the others and that was volleyball. Still a passionate sport of mine even today, it was the closest social interaction with peers and male classmates that I had, other than karate. Before tryouts officially took place, there were open gyms and intramurals. I was sick early on that second semester, so my attendance to those as well as classes took a hit.

March came along and we had tryouts. I was nervous about them. People all knew each other and I only felt as if I was familiar with them. I felt out of my element being around that many dudes because I never had that many people around me outside of the classroom. This was different. The demons played a role in this, not the guys. The coaches were the best and the players I ended up making the team with were fun and I slowly fit in. It felt unnatural but it happened.

My mom even made it out to one game, and my dad did, too. For no other reason than randomness in the schedules, they attended different ones. My dad still boasts even to this day that the only game he got to see me play in was the only game we won that freshman year. I'll be damned!

We did awards at the end of the season. I won the Most Improved Award as I mainly played on the B team, but played some on the A team, too. As the season wrapped up, I went back to my hermit stage. At times, writing and thinking about it, I even come across to myself as if I am making it out to be more than what it was. I stress this point often in this book. Then again, I know that I spent years of acting as if there was nothing wrong with me. It becomes a balance once you are ready and healthy both mentally and emotionally. In high school, I was not there, not at all.

Then, came another summer with having a routine, which was a lack of routine. I had my karate, staying at home, drinking behind my parents back, night terrors, our quasi-annual trip to the Wisconsin Dells and my uncelebrated birthday outside of my family. Wow, I guess it was action packed. I'll be damned times two!

As soon as I turned fifteen, I landed my first job at White Hen Pantry on a work permit from school. Glen & Brenda Aguilar were the owners. They were the best first bosses I could have asked for. I was not lazy, I wanted hours and I had a positive attitude. I got to be someone I was not at school: social, outgoing and confident.

I was a cashier. I would run the register, stock, clean and keep busy. We had a polo shirt for a uniform and a name tag. My uniform always had a smile to go with it because I loved working and making money. Even today, I still do. It is like a release for me, to avoid thinking about what is really going on or what is wrong in my life because I have a job to do or customers to help or a boss to please.

My coworkers became friends, in a short period of time, at least the ones that were not my age. I still had some awkwardness in talking and socializing with my peers even there. Peggy Malcomson was one of the longest tenured employees there. She was a motherly figure but also became a dear friend of mine, still is. She had the same kind of personality and spit-fire attitude like Reba, from her television show.

I remember coming close, twice, to telling her about my eleventh birthday. Peggy was the kind of person I could trust with that, or anything for that matter. Some customers were like that, too. A gentleman by the name of John would regularly come in. Nicest guy on earth. He would have been a close second to Peggy who I would have told. Yet, the secret remained with in me.

Sophomore year was a little bit more fun. I would still avoid the cafeteria. I did not feel comfortable sitting at a lunch table with my friends. I was too shy, embarrassed to be in this scenery. My choice of lunch seating was by my locker, studying and keeping to myself. Then, I would splurge on a calorie buffet when I came home, often in privacy.

Okay, looking back on this part, I may even have to question my sexual preference but there was a whole bunch of girls who had shared the same row or cluster of lockers and would sit by them too that year. I thought to myself, should I ask them to leave so I can be alone and enjoy my privacy?! So, if I sat with all of these beautiful girls, why did I not invest more time or effort in getting to know them better and hang out with them outside of the halls at Neuqua Valley. Yeah, kind of suspect to some I am sure.

I spent a good while just doing me and did not even muster up the confidence to start talking to these girls for the first month or two practically. To this day, I still talk to most of them. They were some of the pretty girls, as if they were out of the magazine or runway. Tan, thin and walked like they were facsimiles of Britney Spears. They were actually even friendly to me. Sure, there was no reason for them not to be nice. Or even more, there was no reason for me to assume they would not be nice. Lunch was fun because I never heard more conversations about relationships, chick flicks, periods, bras, parties, etc. my life. I felt like I was on the juniors' edition of 'The View.'

I never once thought of asking any of them out, or even to do something social outside of school. I had my own life outside of Neuqua: karate, dancing to TRL, drinking alone, playing volleyball and watching Rollerjam. I could I fit in hanging out with girls. If in front of the mirror, upon comparison, I thought why would they be interested in me; I was not attractive, I was too skinny, my hair?, my face?, my pale skin,? my mild acne???

I could write a grocery list of the reasons why these girls would not want to be my friends outside of lunch or school. However, knowing how genuine they were and still are, in addition to the demons that played in my psyche, they could probably come up with a list of reasons why they would hang out with me, just as long.

Homecoming of my sophomore year was another school dance not attended. I just plugged away at my studies. Karate was still the thing for me and I had my job. The holidays soon roamed and I got sick that year. It was from then on I feel like I have always notoriously been ill for any period of time between November, like around Veterans' Day and February, close to Valentine's Day (both Single's & Colorblind Awareness Days for me).

In any event, spring semester came along. The cast of girls at lunch near my locker changed just a little bit. I was gearing up for volleyball tryouts and still working away at White Hen Pantry. There was one night, in January of that year, 2001. I remember waking up on a Sunday night to head downstairs. I took the beer I saw in front of me. My mom and dad had plenty of it as it was the 'Super Bowl' that night.

I took a stash and opened it up in the garage. That became the scene of me drinking, popping open each top so I can get drunk. Never before did I get drunk. This night was different. I think I was out there for close to sixty minutes, chugging away at the cans. Bud Light was my date that evening. But a rude threesome occurred as my flashbacks of my eleventh birthday arrived. I struggled to sleep. Even after retiring and putting away the beer that I had, placing the evidence in the trash next to my parents seemed strategic. My habits of covering up my tracks were meticulous and almost precise. I brought one can up with me as a night cap, like that cigarette after sex. This last bud light was potent compared to the rest as I feel asleep right away.

In the morning, I woke up for school with a headache, feeling sick. It was my first hangover. It was not as glorious as the movie with Bradley Cooper and cast had made theirs out to be. Nonetheless, my mom bought into me being sick and not hung-over. It never happened again as I do not see how people loved that feeling in the morning. Though, that would change in college (wink, wink!).

Later that week, my mom found that last can hidden in one of the cabinet doors to my wooden entertainment center. I played it off like as if I thought it was a can of root beer and did not want to get into trouble for taking a beer. Problem averted as that excuse worked. After all, I had good grades, a job, was still doing karate. I did not fit the bill for an underage drinker.

That moment, I almost seized the opportunity to retract my lie and tell her the truth, the whole truth. I came down the stairs, about to bring it up and then I feel short, again. 'Ankle-Deep' was as far as I was getting with telling her, or anyone. Something that happens in such a short time frame, a matter of minutes, can haunt and alter a child's life for so long, all just from harboring it in.

The feelings of shame, guilt, remorse, as well as embarrassment and disgust for myself were resonated deep into my mind and heart. There was very little that I felt proud of when I was alone, but in front of others, I was happy. Truth be told though, I was alone more times than not. The struggle of pretending and accepting myself for who I was or am, also added to the demons.

I tried out for the volleyball team again, this time falling short of making the team. I was asked by Coach Roberta Daniels to stay on as a Manager. I said yes. I got to practice and be around the same group of guys with a few new additions. The decision of me accepting was a surprise because I put myself in a position of being around my peers, around dudes my age on a regular basis just because.

It was a fun season. The guys on the team, Rudy H, Ryan B, E.J., Jim G., Greg R., Dan F., Nick D., Alex D., Kyle D, Brendon O., Alex O., Mike K. and Ed T. There was this habit of mine to avoid the stretching and warm ups. Part of it was to minimalize my time around the guys, to avoid getting close or team bonding. I felt embarrassed and lesser around them. The other part was half laziness. I would talk to other teachers or visit the school counselor. I would be seeing the people I should but not doing anything productive with them. Avoidance at its finest.

My mood would change during the season. I would shell up because I had so much on my mind. It was no longer my thoughts and horrors regarding my eleventh birthday. It became the indescribable feeling of loneliness and depression. I thought I was ugly, thin, pale, unattractive, annoying, weak, and more . . . or by comparison of those adjectives, less.

During the season, Coach Daniels had even approached me in the hallway before practice on day. She, too, was running late, by coincidence. She had asked me a serious question. Her question was a probing one in nature, but very genuine. Coach asked me how come I had my moments or days where I was down and seemed unhappy. Truth be told, another opportunity was merited and also forfeited by me to tell her the full truth.

I did not tell her the truth, obviously, as I elected to not break the cycle. It became habit or routine to cover up what was going on. I told her that I was ok. It was just the typical high school stress and nerves that come with the territory. Seemingly, she went with it but I know she knew better. I could tell she had a watchful eye on me.

It happened again with some of the guys from the team. E.J., Alex D. and Dan were there. I think Ben B, from some previous classes who was friends with these guys, too, also was there for this moment or exchange. It was in the hallway next to the locker rooms and gymnasium, coming from the cafeteria. The same question came up again.

Botched and flawed were my efforts to open up. I still possessed this level of fear and shame in sharing that I was molested earlier in life, knowing that I was not 'normal.' Upon writing this chapter, I realize how much more alert about the effects and aftermath it had. I underestimated my own comprehension in my adolescent and teenage years.

E.J. led the conversation stating that I was one of the nicest kids he knew. He added that I was good person, who made a lot of people laugh and that I was friends with everyone in our grade. He was probably the one person from the volleyball team I felt most comfortable sharing my secret with. Alex D. was a close second.

I remember excusing myself to use the restroom, but it was an exit path as I spent a good while crying before the game would start. I was pouring out so much emotion. Fear, anxiety and shame were finally accompanied with relief, hope and faith that I could get through this. Just knowing what people thought of me and it being positive was the greatest gift of all that year.

At the time, E.J. dated this girl named Hilary W. Ironically, Hilary and I became closer friends than E.J. and I were after high school. But nonetheless, she was super nice and always polite and friendly, especially with me. I remember confronting E.J. in math class about why she was this way with me. He told me it was because I was a nice guy and that he and I were friends, trying to assure me that there was nothing behind it.

From here on, my manners were lacking when someone would try to pay me a compliment or try to plug or promote me to their friends and family as E.J. did. I could not handle or accept a compliment. It was too boastful in my eyes because I never agreed with it.

Unless I was having a really, really, really good day, but those were few and far between.

Looking back on it, as I do from time to time, I acted like an ass in those moments. I sheltered something that was not so big to me at times, but in others was so huge. By not so big, I mean that I created a vortex of pain and suffrage by not being honest and open. Honest and open is who I have worked at becoming and always been considered by almost all of my peers, teachers, coworkers, bosses and family. So for one particular instance or circumstance of my life, it crippled the very fiber of character that I prided myself on most. There lied the greatest source of my pain.

The season wrapped up and I thought it would just fade into another end of the school year, lead into summer segment. Much to my surprise, a pleasant one at that, came to me as a token at the awards ceremony to end our volleyball season.

Our awards for Most Valuable Player, Most Improved and Most Inspirational were handed out. I was given a special award, almost more of a reward. I giant silver star, signed by everyone, saying 'Scottie, You're Our Super Star.' To this day, just thinking about the gesture and act of kindness towards me still makes me smirk, halfway smile and sometimes hold back a tear or two. I had that token for the longest time until it was lost in the move to Evansville (which will be brought up in due time).

I harnessed the momentum of being appreciated, loved and cared for into the summer. I worked again all summer long and kept up with the karate. Yet, the social interaction still was subtracted from my summer vacation. I could have called someone, taken a chance of someone saying sure I'll hang out, or no thank you I am busy. But, I did not.

Instead, my guests were the confinement to my room, the terrors and flashbacks of my attack and the beverage of coping and companionship, beer. I also moved to sampling some of my parents' hard liquor. Vodka and Rum became quite delicious as it was quicker to make me feel tipsy and eventually fall asleep.

Half-Way There

It was a rough entry into my junior year. At work, the Aguilar's (my work bosses at White Hen) were hit with a family tragedy. Their youngest son Michael died in his sleep. It was the last week of August, right before Labor Day Weekend. I was so consumed in work because that was my escape and because my bosses were so good to me. I offered to miss school that week to fill in, until my mother recanted my gesture.

I still was able to attend the funeral. I do not do well at funerals. They have become the setting of some of the few emotional out pours I have exposed myself to are funerals. There is something raw about mourning the loss of someone's life to me. It is not meant to be deemed morbid, but I hate the transition of being happy and appreciative of one's bond with someone alive, then have to automatic embrace their time on Earth while we see them lifeless. That is the emotional logic evoked when I attend funerals that draws the tears and emotional imbalance out of me.

My class load was stronger and tougher, karate became more stressful as teaching classes was at the forefront. There was a man by the name of Bruce Walsh. He was a lead instructor, too. We became close and I felt really comfortable, mature and confident around him; Almost enough so where I could tell him about my 11th birthday until the concept of 'Ankle-Deep' commandeered my thought process.

There was some struggle balancing it all, but overloading my itinerary was a method of me avoiding the pain and suffrage of my past and hiding from the demons that lay beneath the surface.

This is about the time or period in my life that I started feeling down on myself physically in the worst way. I found the slightest pimple or blemish to be a mood changer, or the small things like my weight, complexion or hair to make me feel ugly. There would be classmates, co-workers or peers in general that I would compare myself, too. Openly, I could say another dude is attractive, good looking, regardless of sexual orientation. I would not be attracted to them, but I am not the type of dude to use the disclaimer or descriptor: 'I can see why girls think they are hott!'

To me, I did not have enough appreciation or hold any high regard for myself. Instead, I would value it in others. Of course, I found women to be attractive too, but that is what I was attracted to in high school. Feeling ashamed of what happened to me led me to believe I had a reason to be ashamed in who I am, or was.

I went to a Homecoming Dance for the first time at my high school, with my friend Jill Dailey. She was a friend of mine from when I first moved to Naperville and also rode the bus with me in high school. I had fun, we were pretty close, still talk on and off to this day because of the marvel known as Facebook.

I found pictures to be gaudy and inappropriate for me. I would skip the yearbook photos, taken often during our P.E. classes on a particularly designated day. There was no need for me to be seen if I was not happy with my looks. There was no desire for me to place myself in another vehicle to observe my distain for my own physical appearance.

Close to the holidays, my habit of being sick kicked in yet again. This time, I lost significant weight. I was sick. I forced myself to avoid meals in hopes of losing any imaginary excess weight I saw because I had this fear of being overweight. I was critical of my appearance because of the boys and girls I grew up with. The girls looked like models and many of the dudes looked like body builders or Calvin Klein models. I would be lucky to grace the pages of Kohl's as a sandal or wrist watch model.

By comparison, I viewed myself as inferior and lesser. My nose was the biggest feature that I disliked about my face and body. For many years, my request for a nose job was rebuffed. I would accompany that request with one of getting a tattoo where I would also receive rejection from the parental units. My nose was the staple to the majority of my distain in my physical appearance. It became the blemish in the center of the canvas known as my face.

So my holiday request would be foiled for a fourth straight year to have a nose job. Nonetheless, I went on with my life. Or so I tried. Second semester paid some dividends as I gave volleyball another go. I was not asked back on to play, instead I was asked back on as a Manager, again. I declined and instantly felt rejected, almost offended. I thought my hard work would have paid off and I was let down.

I remember ignoring Coach Daniels for a number of weeks, almost a month and a half probably, during my lunch option as she monitored the part of the hallway where I sat by my locker. By the time I rejoined the group of people I knew familiarly well and even was honest about my stand-offish behavior towards Ms. Daniels, all was normal again.

An honest moment with a classmate, someone I do, or did consider a close friend by default was Ben B. Ben asked me one day, bluntly but genuinely, 'How come there are days you just seem unhappy man?' Instantly, I almost jumped at the opportunity to pull him aside one on one and tell him the truth. We did not have a lot of interaction with each other outside of school aside from sharing the same friends and being at some same functions. But that particular moment, the fact that someone cared and asked how I was doing, noticing I may not be doing well overwhelmed me.

It is funny how the smallest gesture may come across as more to the one receiving it, as oppose to the view from the giver. That assessment held true to that day. I remember thinking about how to start the conversation. I even called him from my cell phone, which was a car phone looking piece of 'Zach Morris-looking walkie-talkie' sh*t.

He said he already had plans and I deterred myself from trying any harder after that. I have a habit of shutting down sometimes after failure, rejection or anything I interrupt as that. It was not like I cried over it of course. But I took it as he was not interested and move on, but not forward. Because of my negative nature to let things go, accept the positive in life and embrace the good, I held on to many demons, developed some new ones and never really knew how to love myself.

Finding love in other people and things in life felt second nature, but it was a cheap replacement of the real thing since it was not 100% pure. This validates that saying, 'If you can't love yourself, then you can't love anyone else.' I thought I was the exception.

I considered attending prom that year, then decided on skipping my Junior Prom. My focus was on working, karate and wanting to graduate early. I declined and gave myself a chance to do me Senior Year. I thought sure college in California might be the answer, only to realize I was still running away from me. At least, with one more year under my belt, I might make progress.

That whole summer, I built myself up to be the best I could: Social, funny, positive and friendly. I wanted to be comfortable and feel accepted. Perhaps I was all along and had it in my head that just because I did not like whom I was that nobody else did. Today, I accept that statement because I did not accept or like what happened to me August 1st, 1996, that I or anyone else did not like who I was or would turn out to be. Another saying validation with the one about assuming; I know I made an ass out of myself, as it got worse in college. But we will get to that in time . . . wink, wink: foreshadowing.

My father was unemployed fall semester of my senior year. The company he worked for went out of business and he was left without a job for months. It made our family buckle down some, but we managed. Enduring as we were and did, that is a trait we all do well, each in our own way. No matter what, I have always been able to find a job or two along the way, regardless of how close it is to my major or degree. But I would rather work, make money than be picky and jobless; same with my family.

That year, I took the liberty to say what was on my mind, without any filtering. I was the corniest king of one-liners I knew. Iam strictly talking about being that one kid in class who could say something based on the previous statement, comment or question because one word or concept was in common; the literary class clown, so to speak.

In government class, when going over the rules of the presidency, we discussed you had to be born in the United States. I of course thought deeper into that and in raising my hand, blurted out if it mattered where your parents conceived you. Yah, not such a well thought out question when I look back on it.

In Newspaper Class with Mr. Lance Fuhrer at Neuqua, we deemed my habit of blurting something based off of one word that was mentioned in someone else's previous statement. Six Degrees of Scott or 'Scottisms', this habit has not changed but rather just evolved over the years. My many years of watching MTV, E! and VH1 have contributed to the sources of some of the outbursts and clever quick whips as well.

Halloween came around, my favorite holiday. Ashley M. had a nice party at her house with food, beverages, television, costumes and a nice relaxed environment. My costume was my karate uniform. That would be the last of the regular costumes for all eternity as now I take a different route: another foreshadow!

There was no liquor, drugs or anything of that nature as her parents were home and the party was in her basement. It was a nice, legal and appropriate party (Rare in Naperville with this group). I was flattered and humbled she had invited me and it was fun. I returned home at curfew since it was a school night and my mom and I hugged on the living room couch. It was here opening to investigate the smell of my breath. She was searching for booze in my breath. I passed her inspection, duh!

Before finals, I remember I forced myself a break from school and wanted to be alone for a few days. I came home that Friday, being sick. By sick I mean I let myself catch a cold by not wearing a jacket, skipping meals and not exercising. I faked how ill I was in order to be home, by myself for as many days as I could, but pre-arranging it so that I would not miss out on too school work. I would let my teachers know, especially my English teacher, Mrs. Tancredi was back now after Mrs. Klepzig subbed for her, as well as my Calculus teacher Mrs. Colgan.

I got three days out of it. I spent time watching television, going on walks in the cold. I did not have to work those days, I skipped karate. It felt good to take time for me. In all honesty, it has been hard for me to do so ever again because I knew I had lied and deceived a number of people just to do so in order to feel better. Thus, a sense of guilt would surround myself anytime I would ever decide to do take a time-out for me.

The holidays came again and I just remember being miserable. I hated Christmas because at this time I officially was the on-and-off again believer. When I was on, my Faith was strong. When I was off, I blamed God for what happened to me. It really had been like that for two years or more now at this point. I thought many nights to myself: How could God let this happen to me?! Moreover, I still find myself finding small traces of that thought pattern or line of question in my life today.

I spent the rest of break (after Christmas) and a failed attempt to host a New Years' Eve Party, waiting for the last first day of classes, because technically Day One of Second Semester would be just that. My dad was offered a job with Shoe Carnival in Evansville, Indiana. He moved down a couple days after New Years' and he split his time that whole semester. I was never close with my dad by this point but it changed the our home life our family during my senior year. This dynamic added to some of my internal depression, believe it or not: spending my senior year without my father around. Yes, I understood why, but I had had enough of the moving around and changing houses or friends that I could take in my life.

As usual, I would try and switch up my schedule some in high school. I dropped my Spanish class to take an Advertising elective instead, with Mrs. Knuth. I also switched my P.E. period around. My counselor always catered to me and other students the best of her abilities. I should have taken that outlet to talk about me a bit more seriously. Then again, 'should have, would have, could have.'

My parents really forced the college thing on me. 'Where to go' and 'what to study' were the questions of every week it seemed like. Part of me was scared of the concept, as I declined at times, not wanting to go. My mom said 'You have to,' so I started applying to a number of places but Indiana University and Ball

State University were the big two, knowing we were residents of Indiana. Ball State became the selection as IU rejected me . . . jerks! LOLZ!

That Spring Break was spent planning our move. I remember two weeks after having to go down again to house hunt, I asked a teacher during class (Senior English—2nd Semester) what we would be doing to cover. She was snippy at the question as she openly expressed why she did not understand how students and families would go on spring break outside of the designated spring break. I responded without haste in that it was because we were moving and looking for a house where my father has been living by himself the past three months. She instantly said 'Oh!' and had us all head to the library for some research time.

That English teacher pulled me aside to apologize and I told her I was just as sorry for being as blunt and bold with my remark. I found myself being very straight forward with people and not afraid to say what it was on my mind since then . . . well, with the exception of one thing, of course. I hate that it took a nice teacher to say something slightly off for me to become more stern in my life. But puberty kicked in late, I grew some balls and for the next few years they would eventually grow bigger, figuratively of course. Personally and physically it is between me and my doctor or insert current female fling's name here _____.

Leading into April, Prom was the only subject to trump Graduation and College in terms of discussion topics. Because I was on the Newspaper Class Team, I had the inside track to some of the knowledge on Prom Court voting. I was close to the ranks of Prom Court according to our faculty advisor and instructor for this class. I was instantly honored and humbled. Someone like me who was self-viewed as below average actually could be respected by their peers?! I am my own worst critic.

I did not want to attend Prom as I was already focused on the move to Southern Indiana, college and a fresh start. This was the origin of my earliest form of what I deem or term as the 'Bigger, Better . . . Now' Syndrome. From here on, I have developed the tendencies to look forward to the next best opportunity, often jumping past logic or reason and assuming gold always lie ahead and never settling for silver or bronze. I tend to resist the notion of living in the now. I did not take the time to enjoy the last two months of my Senior Year, knowing all too well high school was only temporary, college was the now and my career was my future.

The momentum of me finding the little bit of a voice that I developed carried through at work and karate. I felt less passive but would not say I was fully aggressive just quite yet. However, the ground work to become such a person was most definitely present there. I remember counting the days because I was nervous for moving on but excited to start college and make new friends, perhaps even have a social life. Just maybe Evansville would be the host to some change, some positive change.

Prom Night was close upon me (two weeks or so away) and I asked my friend Darrah C. I went halfway just to say I went but I also went, asking Darrah because I knew we would have fun. I never wanted to be that person who said skipped Senior Prom and accumulated an enormous amount of sympathy whenever I would be asked about it. I had fun, but I knew I could have had more fun if I was comfortable with myself. I felt ugly, down on myself. My date, Darrah, looked amazing: borderline auburn hair, porcelain skin, beaming smile and a pair of gorgeous eyes to match.

I remember making a couple trips to the bathroom, pouring water on my face, on my hair and even using paper towel to wipe my teeth constantly and my face. I was not happy with me, I was never happy with me. It perhaps even ruined Darrah's evening as I disappeared from time to time.

The rest of the weekend was fun, as it was not the typical Senior Prom type where a wild party or raging trip took place. It was just an innocent and lovely trip to The Brookfield Zoo. The train ride was exciting in itself as we quickly learned what stops to never get off on again because they looked straight out of Harlem Nights' dark and demolished side. We arrived at Grand Central Station before taking our next train. A game was invented, 'Cell Phone Marco Polo.' We would call each other to hear our ring tones and find each other. It was like mobile device hide-and-seek.

I cheated, I hid in a closed down and renovated women's bathroom. I learned that this was a bad decision as there was a bloody wad of paper towels on the floor. The zoo was fun as I took pictures that were loose and lively. I was coming out of my shell somewhat. I had personality that was just hiding behind the demons and negative cognitions. I knew it was time to let them go when college started. The picture of me mounting a statue of a rhino with my pinky in the corner of my mouth, Dr. Evil style, and straddling this structure was quite out of my shell.

Graduation roamed around. We were moving days after Graduation. I was leaving White Hen, leaving my classmates and memories from Neuqua Valley and leaving my friends and extended family to move to Indiana. I was planning on visiting and hanging out with friends from my Prom group to play some volleyball. Ashley and Guil, a few others played with me behind a church off 75th street towards Route 53. It was a sand court behind the building.

I remember my mother making the biggest fuss about me going right before we moved. My own grandmother, Aunt Sue and father all jumped to my defense. They pushed for her to let me go since all of my packing was done and I wanted to have a chance to say goodbyes. My mom used to complain about me not being social enough, then here she wanted me to decline. I think my mother suffers from some of the same anxiety issues that I do. She means well, always has. We just differ, it causes conflict often.

The ride down was entertaining with my grandmother and I in one car. Just her and me; it was most enjoyable.

Picture a mix of Sophia Patrillo from The Golden Girls and Karen Walker from Will & Grace. Then, there you have a perfect description of my grandmother. A 45 some year old woman trapped in an 80 some year old body. If I told you her age, I would probably receive the heaviest priced lawsuit for libel from her but she is my grandmother and I love her. I think she would forgive . . . if we settled out of court.

We pulled up to the house, after a six or seven hour drive. The house was bigger than the one in Naperville. I looked at that as a silver lining. I also saw my room with two closets. That was symbolic to me, as one could not be enough to contain all of my skeletons, actually just one of them. (For those of you who know me, I know why you are laughing about the closet reference, HAHA!)

I found myself in yet another new state, another new town, starting over and trying to assemble my life as a growing, maturing adult. Doing so without the proper mindset and level of confidence or self-esteem in myself would prove to be a rather difficult and interesting conundrum.

<<< CHAPTER THREE >>>

MOVE TO EVANSVILLE / BSU

*Our deeds still travel with us from afar, and what
we have been makes us what we are."*

—George Eliot (1819-1880) British novelist.

Barely a week in, I was already bored because I was ready to start working. I applied to a few places. It came down to Old Navy and Eddie Bauer in the end. I chose the latter of the two as I wanted something opposite from young and popular to avoid people my age. So much for the fresh start?!

I would work hard, impress my bosses, make some work friends and be content with the new situation I was in. This would be the start of me really accepting that feeling of being content and not only convincing myself it was happiness, but settling for it.

Orientation for college at Ball State University was the only true highlight of my summer. I went back up to Naperville only once during the summer, which ended up being the first weekend we moved. I still made it to a couple Graduation parties.

Ball State University was to be my new home away from home away from home. I never accepted Evansville, or Newburgh (until now), rather, as that is where I was from, then. I still claimed Naperville, Illinois as my home. Even on my name tag at Orientation, I had that on their. But it was funny because my mom had Newburgh, IN on hers. That raised some eyebrows in addition to questions as if I was a child of divorced family in the midst of joint custody, or something of that nature.

I was upbeat about orientation. I knew no one from my high school was there so I did not have to worry as much about what people thought of me. My roommate for the two days was a guy by the name of Shaun or Shawn. I am just certain it was not Sean. In any event, he kept me up all night talking about South Park and other Comedy Central programming and video games. These were three things I did not enjoy talking about nor did I even came remotely close in even pretending I knew what he was talking about.

Karma struck back and he struggled the whole day through orientation trying to stay awake. My mom asked me what happened and I said I am use to staying up all night and being just fine in the morning after quite a few all-nighters I had pulled in high school in order to stay on top of studies and given my anxiety.

Our orientation group clicked really well. In fact, to this day, I am still friends with a number of those people. The first friend I met in it was Jack B. Gosh, the funny thing is my mom and his dad had been very social.

Neither of them cheated or had an affair, but their son's college orientation would be a classy choice of scenery for one if I ever participated in such a deviously sexy activity.

Jack and became friends almost instantly. Amanda H. was also in our group, she rounded out our trio in our group. There was also Natalie W., a tall skinny model looking girl. I think my mom even admitted she was beautiful. She and I are still good friends today. The same is with Paul B. from the group. He is one of my closest friends even today.

A few others like Dominque B., Ian K., Heidi C. and more were with us for the tour and adventuring, too. I remember being the kid known for wearing blue Nike shorts and a white and blue striped oxford with my sleeves rolled up along with tennis shoes. People had their opinions, they were mixed. But I liked it. I found dressing up and clothes were a comfort with me. Sometimes it is about labels but just picking out something and being self-conscious about my attire and wardrobe helped make me feel something.

We selected our classes out and I stuck with the basics. Though I know wanted to do Advertising, I just stuck with the easy freshman year and socially friendly planner. I did not have to work my freshman year, either. My parents were planning on wiring me money as needed.

I did not have a pre-determined or pre-arranged roommate when orientation came. In fact, I was a late applicant and was lucky enough to find out by the end of summer that I was living in Studebaker West, 2nd Floor.

My birthday came around with no one outside of my house to even celebrate it with. It was the most uneventful birthday to date, yet it did not matter to me as much because I was about to celebrate something bigger. I am about to get my degree from a college.

The first semester began smooth, I would have to say. I did not get home sick, but I quickly missed being around the same familiar faces that I did in high school.

My roommate, Dan C., was also from Pennsylvania. He majored in Music Production I believe and was a good roommate. He was cleanly, polite and caring. He had a couple friends on the floor from the year before as he was a sophomore.

I was no longer afraid to set up hangouts or ask people to go to lunch with me. That was of course, sometimes with the exception of dudes. I had two lunches the first day with Natalie and Heidi from my orientation group up in my room. I think the guys on my floor took notice but I did not operate like that.

I was the guy who stayed in the first night and did nothing, but the second night I had gone out to a party with my Dan, Marcus and Griffin on our floor. We had a good time. I never drank more than a few by myself (or so I told people), at least not regularly and obviously not socially. I pounded down multiple beer cups from the keg as soon as my $5 bill reached the hands of the owner.

I was fun, lively and entertaining. Of course I would be as there was a stripper poll in the basement. Now, there is no choreography from TRL that taught me that stuff and this is definitely before I ever watched Magic Mike, four times, on mute, to learn a bad *ss routine. I had the martial arts, volleyball and a little bit of gymnastics background in me. That poll became my prop and I owned it. Nothing fancy went on but I could get some lifts and holds in there for my skinny frame.

There is an old rule in college drinking though: 'What goes in, must come out.' I had to pee, but the bathrooms at the party were either busy or out of order. So I decided it was best to boulder-dash down Marsh Street and run back to the dorm. I signed in and swiped my ID, making it up the stairs to the bathroom. By the time I pulled down my zipper and opened the door to the stall, I pissed all over myself.

I made the mistake of just throwing my pants in the hamper and leaving it sit all weekend until my roommate Dan asked why the room smelled like piss later that Sunday evening. I was open and honest with him about my debauchery, admitting to my drunken antics.

Classes were going good. I liked them all on Monday, Wednesday, Fridays, but my Tuesday and Thursdays were not as pleasant; I had Psychology and Economics those days. Sociology 100 with Dr. Mellisa Holtzman,

Theatre 100 a man I can't believe I am failing to remember, and English 101 w/ Mr. Neely were how I started and ended my week.

Paul B. was in my English and Theatre class. Heidi and Amanda from orientation were in my Sociology class. I met a few friends in my other classes but it was mainly through the dorms and parties I got to meet people.

One fixation I had that helped me meet people was sand volleyball outside of the dorms. I had experience so I shined. I had the Andy Roddick type power serve, though it did not make me millions or win me anything of importance except for maybe an icebreaker or subject matter to talk to people, both guys and girls at college.

There was a group of girls in the dorms from the 7th floor that I met, Amanda B., Rachel C., Nicole B., Valerie S., Melissa D., Renee A, Christine M., Erica (sorry I do not remember her last name, but she was roommates with Amanda) and a few others. We all even went to the first Football game of the season together.

We ate dinner before that at The Atrium and I ran into Jack for the first time. College at Ball State was all about degrees of separation, events, classes, dorms and parties. That is how I met so many people and with my superhuman memory, it became easy for me to be known or at least feel popular.

A pair of girls in my Theatre and English class, Melissa B. and Lindsay S., were two really good friends of mine. We were super close, but even today, we still talk some. There were a few guys in these two classes that I also met and became friends with. Kyle R., who I invited to some parties with us, Zach K. who I had nailed down wrong. I thought he was a preppy asshole, but I was only half wrong, hah he was a little preppy (Got ya Rap Scallion!). These two guys and Paul were three of my best friends and even today are some of the closest people to me.

At one point that first semester, my drinking and partying became so bad that Melissa, Lindsay, Paul, Zach and Kyle staged a mini intervention, putting me on the spot. I quickly got sharp with them about it, defensive in nature and shut them down about it. Though it may have silenced their voice on the matter, it did not slow their thoughts of concern for me. It would later come up again each year in some way, shape or form. They have seen me battle my demons. A few other new friends at this point would join as the audience to some liquored-up instability: Shawn McC, Hilary A., Katelyn B. and Brian E.

In fact, one party up at Purdue that some of the girls from the 7th floor and Kyle, Jack and I drove up to was where I told these two guys what happened to me on my 11th birthday. I am certain the alcohol was the biggest rationale behind my decision to share but I honestly had no regrets. There was no discussion about it. Both shared their opinion on how unfortunate that was and how sorry they were. On the inside, all I could feel or think is how sorry I was picking them to share that and choosing to do so there.

Everything else about my life slowly leaked out and I was an open book. I was a decent student but loved the bottle. Beer or liquor was good with me. My wine phase never came until after college. I opened myself up to new people, made lots of friends. I tried being different or at least being different from the bad habits of self-preservation I exhibited from my previous school days. It is hard to change overnight or even over the course of a semester or two, but I was slowly on my way.

There was an activity I picked up that I had no experience with myself but knew that people in high school did for part recreation and part dependency. That little friend was cocaine. I had snorted cocaine a couple times in college before being completely open and honest about it with Kyle, Zach, Jack, Melissa, Paul and the gang.

I used once or twice at a party around Halloween, my favorite holiday, of course. I decided to up the efforts of feeling in party mode. I became addicted to it to some extent. I did not crave it but I enjoyed the way it made me feel. It made me feel a little more alert, confident, proud and no longer ashamed of my past. It was like a Jeckyl & Hyde complex. Naturally, my friends expressed their concern. I stopped snorting, I did not use cocaine: at least temporarily.

The same trend of being sick in November/December still was in affect and I used that as an excuse to miss some classes, mainly on Tuesdays and Thursdays. It was my time to be alone and think about stuff. I think the time period of me quitting coke triggered my immune system. It is amazing how you can feel so alone in your life sometimes and yet, you find yourself surrounded by people and have multiple aspects in your life to keep you entertained.

I still had my demons battling the way I looked at myself physically. I made people laugh, I was nice and kind and fun, but never took in anything positive about my appearance. I struggled with this for years. More of the same from high school, it was like being stuck in a yearly cycle without knowing what is going on or how to prepare for it. The feeling of emotional and mental bewilderment took over.

So I turned my attention to partying because I knew beer and liquor made me feel better. At parties I would make more of an effort to flirt, court and advance with women. I was never forceful, I was polite. But I wanted the physical companionship. After all, I was an eighteen year old boy who was away at college.

There would be girls I made out with, fooling around with as my sexual nature was explored. I am electing to say now, instead of earlier, I lost my virginity in High School, freshman year and chose to re-abstain, better known as 'Born Again Virginity.' Only, I would leave out the first two thirds of that concept or title (Born-Again).

I did not have sex again until a party during the holidays with a girl that I had some small history with. It remained simply plutonic, on and off for some time. I remember being open about after a friend in college asked me about sex and virginity considering their own history. To avoid disclosing their name and story I converted it into my own as if to find others opinion about double pump and out and whether it still counted. I took some heat but I did it to protect that friend.

Loyalty was one of my biggest attributes. I mean I was not used to having close friends, especially guy friends. So I would not mind taking a bullet for anyone of them, as I know they have done so for me. In fact, many of them probably still do even today.

Wrapping up a first college year of partying, making friends, C+/B—average GPA and just beginning to get into my own confidence and maturity, I came back home for summer. I started working at Shoe Carnival across from the mall as a cashier. My dad worked in the corporate office for almost a year and a half at this point. From here on out, for three summers, they hired me on for summer help.

I met a number of people and they knew about me playing volleyball or being from the Chicago area or that I went to Ball State. We would all play sand volleyball at Wessleman's. That was one thing I looked forward to, as we mainly played on Sunday nights. It would often be with or against people from Old Navy, too. Funny how that store keeps coming up in my life!

A friend of mine from high school came down to visit in late June for a couple of days. He discovered some cocaine in my room and was pissed off. I found it hypocritical because he used also. I found him to be disappointed in me and even after some time had went by, over the years, that friendship just deteriorated.

I began a habit of rejecting established friends because they were too close. I turned back to the cocaine for some confidence, some entertainment during a mostly boring summer. Sure, I hung out a lot with some people from work like Shaun W, Erin W., Julie Y., Taryn F. and some others. We mostly played volleyball and would drink a few times with each other. But I often kept to myself and stayed in my room whenever I was not working. I did not have a car to drive after two stellar accidents I got into in high school. So I was often stranded at home, barring the exception of some rides to and from work or volleyball.

One of the few highlights was having my guy friends from Ball State come down to visit: Zach, Paul, Kyle and another guy, Christian V. He had played volleyball with us and was friends with my second semester roommate, Brad K..

Jack was unable to come down, but the weekend was still enjoyable. My mom had even told these friends after I left the living room that it was so important to me that they came down here because I was struggling down here. She knew about a decent portion of the drinking but I do not think she knew of my cocaine use. The depression was obvious but the source was not to her, nor to a lot of other people.

After that weekend wrapped up, I had just a month left before Ball State resumed its classes. I was anticipating my return as if it felt like years away. I viewed this house to harbor so many of my demons and darkest thoughts.

My birthday had a little more celebration this year, though it came with more pain and agony in some dreams and isolated thoughts. I still could not shake some of the terrible things that happened. It drove me to drink some more. I had become a borderline functional alcoholic and chemically dependent. I would spend money on both, booze and coke. Sometimes I came in to work hung over or still under the influence of either or both.

Looking back on it, yes it is stupid to do drugs. I do not condone it. Chemical dependency is common in victims and survivors of Child Sexual Abuse (CSA). According to Darkness 2 Light, a non-profit organization that supports the awareness and prevention of CSA, the statistics for substance abuse following CSA are evident. 'The consequences of child sexual abuse often follow victims into adulthood. Most people have no idea that the effects of child sexual abuse are so pervasive in adult life.'

In fact, 'male adult CSA victims 2.6 times more likely to report substance use problems (65% versus 25% in general population), (Simpson and Miller, 2002).' Furthermore, 'Female adult survivors of child sexual abuse are nearly three times more likely to report substance use problems (40.5% versus 14% in general population), (Simpson and Miller, 2002).'

But, today I view myself as more than just a statistic. I am a survivor. My testimony only further validates the norm established in our society as a result of this growing epidemic of horror and terror. By my 19th birthday, I would say I was an alcoholic and full blown addict. A functional one at that, but nonetheless, I had established a chemical dependency problem to help cope with or at least mask my demons.

The new semester started out strong. I even ran into a familiar face from Neuqua who evidently transferred to BSU that semester. Her name was Laura H., now Lani C. There is something about a Naperville connection, I do not miss a beat with them. My mom was even in town for the night to visit on the Monday of Homecoming.

A big group of us went out to Applebee's for one of the girl's birthdays from the 7th floor the year previous. They all now lived off campus. Lani and I clicked as if we had been friends since first grade. Though we had similar friends, we had one class, Spanish, that freshman year and that was it. She is married now, to Nate Cameron. They both are amazing people, genuine in nature.

They are fun loving and have their sh*t together. They are people you look up to and yet still motivate me to do what I am working on or accomplished. I can honestly say that I have never had a falling out with her or Nate and never experienced any level of drama with them at all.

I met some more friends, Megan S. and Adam C. Two people, who at the time were dating, were two of the closest people to me. The three of us even went out for Halloween and would hit up parties often. This was the first year I developed a habit of living my life one day precariously through another person's life. As I grew disgusted with myself, I viewed Halloween as an intoxicated departure from my mess. That year, I dressed up as Andy Roddick.

My costume consisted of a white t-shirt from Hollister that said 'I Play Dirty' that I wore over a teal polo. I wore cargo shorts with a tennis ball that I cut in half with each piece super glued to the butt of my shorts. My tennis racket adorned a picture of Roger Federer with an 'X' through it. I utilized the free or discounted tanning coupons from the dorms as well, in order to complete the costume.

For the majority of one week, I felt special. People took notice, they loved my costume, the whole outfit. I felt like they loved me. I am both honest and comfortable to say, that even today as well as back in 2004 that Andy Roddick is hott. So when people noticed me then as Andy Roddick, I felt hott for those decorated days of Halloween parties.

I got sick just a bit when I was trying to cut back on my partying after that Halloween. I lasted about a month or two, a celebratory but temporary duration for my sobriety. I relapsed and kept it private until I had developed some further health issues that fall semester of my sophomore year. I was hospitalized for a liver infection, gall bladder infection and jaundice. My red blood cell count was through the roof and I also was diagnosed with mono.

My studies and my health took a hit. I saw myself lose some weight. My drinking still persisted. I missed a lot of work. I eventually quit my job up in Muncie because of an incident where a manager I suspected of stealing was singling me out and retaliated against me. She would eventually be fired for guess what, stealing and I was never dignified with any type of apology.

The holidays came close and I was in my first serious relationship, with a girl named Nikki K. She was a year younger than me, living in the dorms only a floor above me. We met through an event in the dorms that I helped put together. I was involved in Hall Council to some degree.

The event was a remake of 'Singled Out' from MTV. It was the dating show that put Jenny McCarthy and Carmen Electra on the map. That is how we met and it was short lived. She was pretty, upbeat, fun loving, focused and had the go-to features I still look for today. Nikki had the contagious smile, gorgeous eyes and great sense of humor.

Along with any other relationship, I only went 'Ankle-Deep' with her. My demons got the best of me and I knew I was not ready to commit. Today she is married to a guy named Joe. Nikki still is an amazing girl I am sure as the genuine diamonds never change their shape or form.

The holidays came around the corner. I did not even go home for Thanksgiving, I visited Jack up north as he did not return to BSU the next year. I avoided Evansville as much as possible. I was a nomad in every sense of the word.

Christmas I came back but I did not enjoy myself. I remember coming back to BSU with yet another roommate. Though there was no particular falling out with any of them; they either just transferred or moved in with other friends, it still added to my self-consciousness of what is wrong with me.

That semester I was all over the place. I met a couple friends from volleyball, one in which I became closer with than the other two. Bill C., Jeremy B. and Hilary W. They were fun, a year younger than me. Bill was actually from Woodridge, Illinois, close to Naperville and my grandma's new house near Darien.

I would play bartender for some mixers and parties and we just became incredibly close. Volleyball, parties and some left over time allocated for studies. This was all a distraction from any demons I wanted to face. They never really came up this time of year because I was preoccupied.

I became distant with Christian, who was probably one of the closest friends I made that year. He lived across the hall from me and closer to Zach. I was more open about everything except me being molested. I may have stated it to him but never discussed it. It was like I controlled what I wanted my friends to know but never what they should or rather what I needed them to know.

Towards the second of the semester, there were two big changes in my social or private life. I had a falling out with Christian, who I could not even tell what the catalyst of it was. The second change was that I met a girl, named Tracy.

I own up to being the type of person who ditched friends or moved on from bonds rather abruptly. Regardless of my demons, it takes a strong person to be friends with me, so I am sure half of it was that Christian did not want to deal with what I had going on anymore. Today, we still even talk and catch up, so we are cool now. In fact, he is also writing a tell-all, self-help book. His is geared for the male audience on the dating world. I have read some of his manuscript and it is clearly entertaining, accurate and worthy of your time . . . plug, plug!

Then, with Tracy, we just were very social and friendly, trying to test the waters. Half of it was timing in the semester, but we stayed in contact with each other over the summer a lot and were ready for the next school year. I definitely was attracted to her. She was very pretty and bubbly.

I focused more on volleyball intramurals, partying, socializing almost more than my studies. I tried out for this Co-Ed Modeling Dance Troupe that my friends Paul, Natalie and Dominique were in. It was a student organization through the Multicultural Center.

I was one of the only Caucasians there. It was merely an observation that did not bug me at all. It did not shun me away. My reservations were my confidence of saying 'I am a model who can dance.' The closest I ever came to this declaration in my own abilities was doing the dance to 'Bye, Bye, Bye' in the mirror wearing my Starter jump suit and Aviator sunglasses.

Surprisingly, I held my own. I made friends, though mainly with the ladies. Hey, nothing wrong with that. Asiah M., Ayesha F., Krystle S. and more were the girls I stuck around outside of Natalie & Dominique.

I remember our first show. I was supposed to be modeling for the fitness or swimsuit scene one. James 'Hustle' Scott, one of the dudes from the Troupe was joking with me saying 'Man, you need to do some push-ups all night if you wanna' look right for this one.' I am not lying to you. It got in my head so much it is probably one of the few weekend nights I ever traded drinking for exercising. I stayed in my dorm room and did a couple hundred push-ups, tricep dips and sit-ups without exaggeration.

I even openly admitted it the next day at the show. It made people laugh. By nature, I could poke fun at myself and be humorous about it. The idea was entertaining, even to myself. It helped me not think about the negative and let it consume me. Yet, instead, I allowed this coping mechanism to focus on how to laugh it off or away.

I earned the respect of the Troupe to the point where I was even elected an officer on the Executive board for the next academic year. My mom, sister and grandmother attended the show where that announcement was made, too.

My grandmother, with that previous description of her still being true, made some noise at the show. It was common to hear the ladies of the front five or six rows to shout and cheer for their friends and familiars on the stage. My grandmother, Nana, did not understand why they said it the way they did.

'I see you Ayesha,' and 'Okay Natalie, get it!' were often shouted from those girls. My grandmother would express out loud in words, 'what is there to get,' and 'of course you see her, Ayesha is on stage.' My mother even reacted slightly embarrassed but mainly entertained by the scenario.

I know those girls laughed too and slowly simmered down on some of the cheering and vocal support until I hit the stage and she yells 'I see you Scott, get it!' All was well in the world again.

After two years of college, I had met a core group of friends, been very close with a number of them, even started dating girls a bit more seriously than I did in years past. I accumulated some confidence in myself, even participating in a Co-Ed Modeling Dance Troupe. Thank god for TRL and self-tanner.

Just perhaps, I found myself coming into my own, about to turn a corner in my life and feel normal. Though I had no example or instance of what 'normal' was to compare it to, I did not feel as low or dragged down as I had in years past. The terrors and nightmares of my attack were few and far between.

My focus now was getting through another boring summer in Evansville and trying to gear up for the second half (give or take a semester or two . . . or three) of my college tenure. Maybe I had it in me to go at least 'Knee-Deep' or 'Waist-Deep' from here on out.

<<< CHAPTER FOUR >>>

MID SUMMER NIGHTS DREAM PARTY

"If your religion does not change you, then you should change your religion."

—Elbert Hubbard (1856-1915) U.S. writer and publisher

Another year, another semester, another living and roommate situation came upon me. My roommates were Kyle R. and two of his friends, Dave Z. and Austin M. They all were from the same school or area from before college. Both of them were a year younger than Kyle and I. The roommate situation was never really an issue compared to what I had going on.

I moved in early, mid-August, and hung out with Tracy, who lived on Marsh Street. Her and I had talked a lot over the summer and was a spark between us. We definitely had some chemistry, short and brief in terms of its duration, but strong nonetheless. We ended up going to Wal-Mart, ate, watched a movie and caught up. There was chemistry there but you can tell she was hesitant on a relationship, too.

Then the next night, I met up with Lani who also moved in to a house on Marsh street. We did the same, met up at Wal-Mart, did a little shopping and then went back to her place to chill. Story of my life, by mere luck or coincidence, Tracy and Lani were neighbors. I told Lani about it and I introduced the two. For almost two years, they were friends, even lived together the next year. I then introduced Lani to my roommate before my party to Kyle. They were friendly and spent some time together. It kind of went kaput and ended the same way and in the same time frame as Tracy and me (But not until after my late 20th birthday party which I had been planning since the semester previous).

Despite being as organized and O.C.D. as I am with my life, I would end up being terrible with money and spending it for the next three or four years. My parents gave me the money from my student loans to also balance with my rent payments at Windermere Place Apartments, off campus at Ball State.

I decided to throw a party for my belated 20th birthday. I made it huge, spending some of the money I was given to pay rent for the semester on this party and clothes and other material objects. The theme for the party was 'A Mid-Summer Night's Dream,' which I openly borrowed from Playboy and Hugh Hefner. Everyone would attend in their lingerie and sleepwear as I made the girl-guy ration close to 4:1.

All of the friends I had accumulated were there, for the most part. I played bar tender again for my own party. I wanted to look extraordinarily amazing and hott for my party. I even went to two tanning places that day of, hours before hand to look dark. I did, but it was stupid and dangerous to do that to my body. I was not using cocaine anymore, I was probably six weeks clean at this point and did not use again until over Christmas break.

I ordered some catering from Panera for the party, spending close to $1,000.00 on the party altogether. I had liquor upon liquor upon liquor. People wore the appropriate theme attire. It was fun. I mean just about everyone was there. For once, I could say I enjoyed my birthday, despite me being tardy with the celebration.

It did not matter, though. I was with friends, feeling good about myself, until about 1:30 a.m. when I am in just a pair of white volleyball compression shorts, throwing up in the toilet. However, the amazing fact is that even as sick as I got, I still woke up at 8:30 a.m. in time for a sand volleyball tournament with Zach.

Zach and I were signed up for a two-on-two tourney and almost won the first match. I was sweating so much liquor, you could smell the tequila, vodka and rum beads rolling down my skin. Kudos to me on my dedication for volleyball though!

That would be the start of a wild junior year. I liked my classes, liked my apartment. I still played a lot of volleyball. I met James W. through Lani at another party early on. This was about the time she met Nate and I was introduced to April C. through James. This rounded out my closest group of friends for the second half of my college life.

Even today, they remain my closest friends. James, Lani and I would always compare ourselves to the American Idol judges, Randy, Paula and Simon. The only difference was we practically agreed on everything, always seeing things eye to eye. There was never drama or a dull moment. Even with April and Nate around. Kyle was a part of the group, too. However, the other roommates and I had some tension, not drama but tension so it took a toll on the friendship along with my alcoholism that picked up.

During that fall semester I actually turned to Zach, who I knew was religious and a man of Faith and asked for his help in accepting God again. I attended Campus Crusades a couple of times and went to a church a few Sunday mornings with him. I even participated in a Bible Study group with him and his friends at a house off Rosewood.

I met some new people, Adam G., Kyle S. and Andrew B., among others. It was actually one of the guys 21st Birthdays we all went to, at Cheeseburger in Paradise. I was the only one underage, but I was the only lit as I poured an empty travel size mouth wash bottle of vodka into my drinks as no one was looking.

There were signs I had been drinking. My voice got louder, my eyes became bolder and my hands moved more as I talked. I struggled to walk straight. Zach drove me back to his dorm and I crashed on his couch. Yep, I owned it. I said I got drunk and did not mind who knew.

I lost any self-respect I regained. Continuing in Trendz of Essence, the Co-Ed Modeling Dance Troupe, or even playing volleyball, all became doubtful for me. I did not do much to put myself in a position to get better.

As active as I was on my search for Christ, I was only going 'Ankle-Deep' as I secretly cared what people thought of me even in regards to the basic level of being human. I felt like a monster, making mistake after mistake.

I planned on coming back for the holidays both times this year, as the year before I stayed with my friend Jack, who I had a falling out with. I felt like he blew me off for this random new girl he found at BSU through AIM. That is right, AOL Instant Messenger. That is how ancient my days in college seem. We did not talk for almost a year. It would actual happen again, with the same girl. I warned him of her cheating on her. I was right, as that has become a habit or common theme in my life with friends. I am either friends with cheaters and they get caught, ending the friendship or my friend is the one being cheated on and the friendship ends.

I came home for Thanksgiving that year. A few shifts at Shoe Carnival made it worth coming home for the paycheck in addition to the home cooked meals. Before I went home, I went out to a party the weekend before with my friend Bill. We hit up Late Night with my friends Megan and Adam. The four of us had a good time, then Bill and I made our way out to a house party.

This party is where we ran into some girls from volleyball and some of their friends. A couple of them were gay and hit on Bill and I. My luck with women was at an ultimate low and I was talking to this one guy named Clint who admitted he was bi. He was only a year younger than me. He was nice, friendly, dark haired and tan.

We became friends, but never very close. The only thing that came of it was one evening we met up and made out in the back of my Dodge Stratus. My car became a scene of some experimental lip smacking just because I was bored and curious about entertaining the idea that maybe I was gay, or bisexual.

I elected not to tell anyone until after the holiday break. Zach was my first friend I told. His reaction was 'You need to stop kissing boys.' I suppose somewhere in translation it was assumed it was a new and regular activity I participated in with beer pong and public intoxication. But I think it was his way of saying he was comfortable in sharing he knew that it was not something I needed to go out and do because the reason was not valid. Zach knew who I was and knew more about me than I probably ever gave him credit for. The same went for Paul and Kyle, as well as James, April and Lani.

My mom called me one day when I was at the library on a weekday night. She noticed my checking account was low, figured I was drinking a lot more and partying. I admitted to her about being depressed and miserable. I held back on telling her why.

There I realized I lost an identity, I was losing myself as a person. She told me she wanted me to come back home. I told her that would be worse and I would drink more and that my depression worsened anytime I was home.

The holidays were rough that year. I did not really ask for anything. I was beyond help and just turned to my friends at BSU telling them that I was miserable, upset and sad. Never did I expose the truth about why.

That Spring Break I led on to wanting to be different. I still was drinking, but clean from coke for another month longer. I elected to go on a mission's trip with our Bible Study group to New Orleans in the Hurricane Katrina relief.

I opened up to our driver on the trip, though her name is drawing a blank. I think it was Andrea, but do not quote me. Zach, Andrew, Kyle S. and Adam G. were there with others. We met up with girls from Bowling Green University and Florida State University at this church in Sliddell, Louisiana.

It was the first time I went a week without drinking as far as I can remember. It was hard. Zach was supportive but almost too much so I became irritable and moody. Not a rare occurrence or habit for me in this state of being.

There was even a morning after waking up on our cots, when I turned over facing the ceiling I said 'God, I would kill for a screwdriver with breakfast.' Zach whacked me in the mouth without even looking trying to play older brother.

Maybe I looked for that, for someone to be the best friend, older brother. I did not have a tangible or close male figure to look up to. My dad and I had so much distance. The last man I looked up to molested me. I was scared to be let down ever again. I felt let down a lot because I had some expectations in friendships. Zach often said that, I suppose I did. Even today, I still do, just nowhere near as severe or particular as before.

A friendship never came normal, but I was dependent on the idea of having a guy friend that close to me because I had not had one. I have had a girlfriend, many during this time, shared with people, though only a few, what happened on my 11th birthday. But the next big hurdle was to let my guard down and just be a dude with a guy friend. I had too much baggage to let that happen. 'Ankle-Deep' syndrome clearly overrode all of that from happening.

Another Trendz show came around, I was partying with the roommates, volunteered to be the designated driver. I drank a few, took some shots and told my roommate Kyle when he came back to check on me. He respected my honesty about not being sober. The other two roommates were pissed and walked back home. I did not care. Shame on me.

I met up with Natalie, who drove me home to Windermere. I opened up and told her the truth, that I was drunk and worse. That night, I relapsed and snorted at a party. My friend Chris who I snorted with came back to the apartment an hour later with two girls and we snorted in my room. It was the first time I ever used in a place other than a dorm shower, party of my car.

I overslept and was late for the morning rehearsal before the show. CP time does not cocaine people time. The show went on and I was feeling fine. I was hung over, still feeling some of the lines. It was the first time my nose bled from it.

That next week Zach hung out with me before returning home. I remember telling him I wanted him. My goal for the summer back in Evansville was to go see a doctor, work on being clean. It was hard for me. I struggled with sobriety and my religion. Zach was the only one I regularly talked to about it. Kyle was a second, Bill a third, but I never told Bill until the summer.

I recanted my interest in seeking professional help. I had convinced myself it was a sign of weakness. I remember spending that whole car ride in tears coming down to Evansville. My summer was going to be spent with my family I had distanced myself with over the years emotionally, I also was in a house with no positive history or memories for me.

Furthermore, I developed into a full blown alcoholic. I would drink during the day on my days off. Often, my water bottle was full of vodka at sand volleyball with friends. Just weeks before I turned twenty one, I was looking forward to my birthday for the first time in ages, my actual birthday, not a party that would be twenty-some days afterwards.

My friend Zach was going to drive down to visit and hang out for a couple of days before school began and our group all moved in for the fall semester. He had been there for me for a lot and I was glad to include him in my events and festivities I planned with my friends from work and over the summers.

I let my guard down, tuning out the demons, separating my insecurities from my ambitions and highlights. However, it would be short lived. Zach cancelled on me, but told one of my closest friends, Erin. I was devastated. I felt let down, disappointed and embarrassed again on my birthday. The feelings of my past triggered.

Of course, having a friend bail on your 21st birthday is not worthy of a level 4 meltdown, but with everything I had riding on it, it felt fair and just, in fact even more than appropriate. I remember being so fired up and emotional about everything, I left my own party and had my friend and coworker at the time, Valerie, take me home.

I did not want to be around anyone, I was feeling too emotional and too enraged to handle anything in Evansville that week. My decision was clear, to move up early to Muncie. I was living with Kyle R. again, this time in a house. It was on Rosewood, just off of Bethel Avenue. Our landlord's name was Connie, she was pretty nice and good on her follow through, regardless of what it was regarding.

Kyle and Lani took me out for my birthday. All three of us had a good time, a few drinks, nothing crazy. When we pulled out of the driveway to our house, as Lani drove us to Dill Street, a song came on the radio that caught wind of a month prior and fell in love with. Justin Timberlake's 'Sexy Back' was the anthem for the evening.

Kyle and Lani knew me all too well to know that this song would become a new obsession. I instantly fell in love with it, maybe even falling in love with Justin, too. I do not know for sure, but all I know is that song and album saved my life that year, as I am about to continue sharing with you.

The next week, I started at T.I.S. Bookstore as a part-time textbook department associate. I had long hours of training, met new people, impressed the staff and made way into starting a new chapter of my life.

I also began a separate one with my health. I went to visit the same gastrointestinal doctor's office for a check-up, two years after my last infection. Sure enough, I accumulated another one, and it caused for drastic measures. I was sick. I needed to quit drinking, definitely cut back if nothing else. My energy levels were spiked and I was told more about Gilbert's syndrome.

Gilbert's Syndrome is a liver condition that falls into the category of liver disease. If not treated or cared for properly, it can lead to Hepatitis C or sclerosis of the liver. The start of my senior year began with a scare.

Zach coincidentally was living down the street, as he moved in with the two guys from Bible Study. So me being down the street from this group, solidified that I really wanted to make religion a focus on my life.

Classes started and I became friends with Christian again. I switched guy friends around out of a quota for trust. Only a few made the cut, but I switched up who I wanted to hang out with, trust, drink and party with a lot to keep the distance and my guard up. I would put up walls upon walls to keep people out, and the truth away. By this point, there were nights I cried myself to sleep because I could be surrounded by friends and people at any time I wanted to but yet feel so alone.

It was hard to keep a healthy relationship with everyone from the Bible study group, as people were aware Zach and I had a falling out. I again shared with him that his current girl was hooking up and making out with other people the semester before, as a close friend shared. Call it snitching, but loyalty is undefined when you are holding back the truth. Though it may be view hypocritical as I was so comfortable speaking about other people's truth, I could not summon the strength to apply that to my own.

I sucked it up and told him about me being sick and it blew up in my face. It became a separate conversion about us patching things up. I was okay with it either way, because I did not want people close to me anymore.

My past haunted me, now ten years later even, my health hit a snag, I wanted to change me, growing tired and annoyed with the way things were. My habits of pushing others began. I was crying out for help. Depressed and borderline suicidal, I needed help.

I lashed out at Zach in a voicemail the next week bringing an unfair conclusion to things. It ended up being a short two months, around Homecoming when we made up. I had already transitioned into dating a girl named Angie, who I knew had common interest in Zach, but was spoken for by his cheating girlfriend.

I never should have been in a relationship as I had no love for myself. The pain I held onto after all these years had torn me apart and I was clinging to anything that would fill the void of a normal life, which I clearly knew nothing about.

Before the end of the year, I was well on my way to another falling out with Zach, took care of my health, gave up liquor and started another relationship with a girl named Dawn. I was crushing on the Biolife Plasma Center Assistant Manager for quite some time. Finally, we were dating. I stayed close with Kyle, and met some new people.

Travis H., Kyle E. & Brooke B., Brian P. and more had become friends with me through volleyball. I came back to school the next semester after the hospital. I spent the next three months sober, not drinking a drop of alcohol. People still saw me out at the bars being the water drinking designated driver. Even that brought attention to me and caused a fuss as I was open about my health, my past and my life, minus me being sexually molested as a kid.

You know, sometimes, I even think 'Did I make a bigger deal of it that what it really was?' or sometimes my train of thought goes more cynical than that and I ask myself 'Maybe I deserved it?'

Today, I take great solace in knowing that I did not deserve it and yes, it is a big deal to be deprived of your innocence as a child and to have it haunt you continuously in life. I never asked for it. I just did not know how to handle it. By the time I did, most of the damage had been done.

I opened up two credit cards, buying clothes to make me feel better about my looks. I looked into surgery options for my nose to get it smaller, reduced in size.

That year, wrapped up abruptly. I moved out for the summer and lived with Kyle E. and our future roommates for my fifth and final year at Ball State. I got promoted at T.I.S. Bookstore, found a second job at the Classified Ad office for 'The Daily News.'

Here is where I began burying myself in multiple jobs, developing that strong work ethic that I carry even today. If I was clocked in somewhere, making money, I could avoid thinking about the negative. Or rather, if I was scheduled somewhere for a job, I knew I did not have time nor the availability to focus on me and my needs.

<<< CHAPTER FIVE >>>

SUPER SENIOR YEAR & 2008

"If you are not yourself, if you surrender your personality, you have nothing left to give the world. You have no pleasure, no use, nothing which will attract and charm me, for by the suppression of your individuality, you lose your distinctive character."

—Edward Wilmot Blyden (1832-1912)
Liberian statesman

I would enter my super senior year, which was my 5th and final year at BSU, needing to take 21 credit hours to complete all coursework in order to graduate on time. Did I mention this was for both semesters???

Yet another moment celebrated of living through someone else's life took place, center stage in fact. BSU's Homecoming tradition of *Airjam* went on as regularly scheduled, only I was on stage twice for two different performances dancing and lip-synching to my hero and idol, Justin Timberlake. The multiple credit cards I opened to buy clothes and outfits to look like him and the earrings, buzzed hair and attempts to grow facial hair were all symbols of rebellion. It was a rebellion of what, or who, I was and a departure from who I ultimately am today.

Sure, the thrill of performing on stage in front of my peers was exciting, uplifting and joyous. But the manner and presentation was disastrous. I learned the choreography to some performances, incorporated some of my own. I licked the routine the best I could to escape being me for just a few moments.

For one night, I did not have to be a victim of child sexual abuse. That night, I got to be someone confident, attractive, upbeat, fun and entertaining. I was popular, but not all in the good way. I was complimented just as much as I was criticized. The reward to me was that I escaped my past and my present all in one stroke. It's rather embarrassing to admit that I impersonated Justin Timberlake to that extent in college. But when you look up to your hero, you feel a sense of pride. I feed off of pride sometimes because I convinced myself it could take the place of self-esteem and confidence. But it serves as a painful, damaging short term fix. A lesson well learned, I should have stuck with only one performance, not two . . . kidding!

My last year at Ball State University had its own set of highs and lows. I was dating a girl named Ashley from a class. It was not a serious relationship and we both were down for dating other people, or so we said. I am not a fan of an open relationship, but I went with it because it was my way of being with Ashley.

I ignored my feelings and my needs to be the man to one girl that I very much liked. I would not say I was in love with her. The term 'love' is one I struggled with for myself, thus it could be easy to imagine why I held resistance to use it towards others.

That year, I became closer with James and April, Lani and Nate. Kyle R. and I became a little distant. I was roommates with a new Kyle. My roommates and I had some space between us and I even moved out for a brief three or four months around the holidays, only to return in February.

Kyle E. and I were still friends, very much so today. He had left for deployment and I took his room as my room was left open and discovered to be ransacked by the previous occupant, a dude we subleased it out to. He was a back-stabbing, drug dealer, who made the relationship among the rest of the roommates difficult; it seems to be a common theme with another some future roommate.

Whether it is my innate nature to smell bullshit or just the fact I call it like it is, I have learned by now, 2012, to roll with my first instincts, but never my first judgments on people. I would never want to cut on another person, especially when I am working on not cutting on myself. However, the exception should be made for individuals who do not offer any moral character, humility and manners. This is when I prided myself on the interpersonal scope I developed: mainly because of the accuracy factor going for me.

For the most part, all I did was spend my time working, studying, drinking alone. I hid my self-guilt and shame for my past and build on it at the same time.

The holidays were bland, I came home for them. We went to the casino in Evansville, as my grandmother and her second husband Carl came down to visit from up north. I was able to take a break from work, but I missed it. The time off had allow me to think of the horrors in years past so I returned early.

New Years' I went out before Kyle deployed, as I was living across the street during those three or four months. I came over and met his friend Kaja, who is still one of my dearest friends ever. She is a D-I-V-A. I think that is why we clicked, duh!

To replace the job from the newspaper I abruptly left before the holidays, I began working for my friend Dustin at Subway. He was an honest, straight-forward, hard-working, loyal guy. So naturally, it was a good fit. Haha, a job at Subway, being fit . . . never mind! I usually do not force those quite like that, forgive me.

In any event . . . I rolled some of the momentum I gained from random moments of putting myself out there and being me. I found a small trace or hint of being and feeling alive. I think half of that was in celebrating a change that was forth coming: my nose job. That is correct. I, Scott Thomas Sieg, am also a survivor of plastic surgery.

For years, I loathed my nose. The thing was huge. It was the catalyst of my personal list of downfalls. Let's be real here, trust issues or not, with a nose like that, I am surprised I ever made it past second base in my life.

After comparing yourself to celebrities, you become a little vain. I would not easily project that onto others because I recognize respect and decency for others, far sooner and deeper than for myself. Today, it is about the same, hovering around par. Kidding, but yes, my self-esteem took years of time and yes, the nose job did help.

"Wanting to be someone you're not is a waste of the person you are."

—*Kurt Cobain (1967-1994) Lead singer, guitarist and musician of Nirvana.*

In a lack of dramatic fashion too, my healing and recovery was remarkably small. People even gossiped about me getting it, but the size significance and bloody nasal drips were proof in itself. I did something for me, at all costs, including my (partially, at the time) insurance company's. It was a gift for my college graduation . . . I had joked about suddenly wanting to start my Master's if I was not satisfied or if I wanted Collagen or Botox. [I have already established having no filter along with a naughty sense of humor. The coping mechanism of choice by default, is now also my favorite.]

So for the last of the days at Ball State, I spent a nice dinner party with Lani, Nate, April & James. The five us went to Vera Mae's Bistro in downtown Muncie. Later that night, I unraveled as if I were preparing to open up to them all about my secret from my 11ᵗʰ birthday. Instead, out came every little secret, miniscule in relevance by comparison.

I also became close to my boss, Dustin, leaving my duties premature to Finals week at T.I.S. Bookstore. Pam, Stefanie, Tina, Mary Jo and Roxanne, all had been like family to me. The girls in the box, though I had an unfortunate nickname that slipped for them, but in time all wounds mend, of course . . . you dead. But the live ones heal!

Tragedy struck my decision making skills and resume of a clean driving record. I was pulled over for a DUI the day before my tentative graduation date. I also found out that all my classwork was not completed and I was not permitted to graduate and receive my diploma. I would need a couple of courses in the fall to pass, four, barely a full-time session.

My mother, not knowing of the DUI until the middle of that summer, knew of my retakes needed to graduated and forced my hand to complete at USI so I could transfer classes back up to BSU for Fall 2008 Graduation, instead of Spring 2008. Phew!

Getting a DUI?! Scott Thomas Sieg, who swore by using adjectives like 'fudgies' and 'fiddlesticks,' made a bad judgment, while impaired by liquor and endangered lives?! This is not how my parents came down on me, or how I imagined they would. This was my own doing.

That whole summer, I was unraveling, but the drinking did not stop. I just became more secretive and discrete about it. My mom was placing me under her own surveillance in terms of car use, curfew, my 'work schedule' being posted. Upon further review, it helped because I never got another DUI and learned my lesson for years to come.

That May 2nd, 2008 was surely a night I am ashamed of. That was something I had control of, but not being molested. It was then I realized I may be breaking through, or if not, I just beginning to break down.

Again, I had to start from scratch. Other than a few people I previously worked at Shoe Carnival and people I met from sand volleyball at Wessleman's Park, I did not have many friends. It was not like graduating and coming home to celebrate with friends of old.

Instead, it was a bitter and stunning chill of reality that I was alone, did not graduate and had nothing to celebrate, yet. My work was cut out for me. I landed a job immediately, with Old Navy.

Ironically enough, it was the one I turned down the first year I moved to the Evansville area for Eddie Bauer. I made some friends early on, as some of them looked familiar from our sand volleyball days of Shoe Carnival vs. Old Navy . . . now I was a turncoat.

Heather M. was the first friend I made back from college down there. She worked in the mornings with me at Old Navy. Managers Marianne and Natalie also were a.m. regulars, with Linda, Megan and Josh, David and Annette.

A few weeks into summer I met a few other friends from sand volleyball during the weekday evenings: Greg S., Mike P. and Corie B. We always played, often with each other and against other groups of people. I also met Tyler S. then, at first, briefly, now good friends since 2012 when I moved back to Evansville, again.

Sand volleyball is like my Facebook or e-Harmony, except I get poked by a sand castle in my shorts and if I get a match it is usually a pair of wounds, not a spouse: But to each their own. I was good at volleyball, it was like my icebreaker or mecca for meeting people. So, I stuck with it. It would still happen even after 2008.

By the time we all started hanging out and drinking together, we all shared a common interest based on my obsession and sharing of such. MTV's hit show, America's Best Dance Crew, was a concept that captured a number of people's eyes, but it stole my heart. Dancing was one of the few vices I had as a coping mechanism when things got rough in my life.

I heard there was a crew on the Second Season of ABDC, Extreme Dance Force. They did good I thought, but another crew captivated audiences across the nation, including our own at Old Navy and more-over in my group of friends. That group was

Fanny Pak. The talented, fearless, bold to better and yet different approach had fair well for these seven inspirational performers. So much that I reached out to them and invited them to be guests of honor as I worked diligently on getting Dance Marathon at USI for the first time ever, after being involved with the ones at BSU in years previous.

Furthermore, by the end of the season, it was nice to hear back from them, expressing their interest and vote of confidence in my efforts. It was uplifting to know that figures from the television set could be so down to earth and genuine. God Bless Fanny Pak!

During this time, I became closer to these people, both from Old Navy and with sand volleyball. Jen R. & Heather M. and myself all had birthdays that were consecutive, back-to-back-to-back.

The idea of combining all of our birthdays was genius. It put less focus and emphasis on the situation I try to avoid and prevent from sharing. If the birthday party was a joint venture like it was, I did not have to worry as much about my flashbacks or terrors that came along with my reservations in being happy on this day.

We decided to plan a theme party for our celebrated occasion. It was a casino theme. We did an outdoor party at Wessleman's before moving it to Heather's apartment and our friend Cory B.'s place.

A common game we always played, regardless of the reason was Mafia. It's a game that is much like 'Clue' meets 'Heads Up Seven Up.' This was the conclusion to the evening and it was awesome. I just now had to focus on a semester at USI, starting fresh before I would officially graduate and move on from the collegiate chapter of my life.

Four classes, an internship with South Central Radio Group and working at Old Navy . . . it was not enough for me. I met a girl that was new to work before I left Old Navy and tried my hand at a different job. Her name was Keena. I was head over heels for her. Brunette, tan, built like a gymnast and an adorable smile that made you follow suit.

Here I am thinking about it again only as I am writing about it when I realize that I know what I want, but I am not always the best at going after it. Some may call it greed, I think I would call it squeezing in life to make up for time I felt I lost.

I was 23 at the time, with very little relationship success, still in college, living at home, a part-time job, an internship . . . but I wanted the next best thing. A relationship with her was on my radar, but sometimes you can't have it all, at least not at once. Today, were amicable and supportive of each other. But just as soon as I switched jobs from Old Navy to Bob's Gym, the dynamic in my life shifted.

I remember being nervous for the job. It was at a gym, which by the looks of my physical stature, the only 'gym' I ever appeared to have an association is a 'Slim Jim.' My confidence going in was a farce. I was shocked to have gotten the job. I was able to work an abundance of hours, even with school, my internship and figuring me out.

The people I met there I had become friends with. Roxie J., Heidi L., Kelly H., Daniel L., Josh R. & Sonny N. (who to this day is one of my closest friends, along with his family: Cheryl, Kate, Nick B. & Kim L.), Lisa B. and more. I was developing that social life, even becoming more comfortable breaking out of my shell away from work. I had the whole out-going and spontaneous thing nailed down to a T, pretty much the same way I had bottled up my emotions and demons over the last decade at that point.

I had to take care of my DUI case from the spring before back up in Muncie, IN. My friend Greg was kind enough to drive me up there and make a road trip of it. I had a lot on my plate. He and I had become really close and I debated telling him about being molested.

The biggest thing about building myself up, concerning to tell someone about it was that I had no practice in it, at least not the successful transaction of it. I never got to put the words together more than five times, if even that many, after telling Jack and Kyle my freshman year of college.

It is a hard pill to swallow, to trust a new friend and share with them that you have a dark secret that may put a shift in the relationship with any friend. I remember calling Greg before this road trip, a few weeks prior. The phone call was dragged out by my struggle to put syllables together, a skill I do not tend to have troubles with these days.

Greg seemed nervous, anxious, too. I took the high road. Instead of telling him truth about what I wanted to tell him, I used the phone call to share that I was a recovering cocaine addict and was nervous my increased drinking would lead to a possible relapse. Phew! I considered that a victory back in 2008, but it was a departure from what I should have and wanted to share. It would be some years later after a falling out that I finally shared that with Greg, about my 11th Birthday.

The holidays rolled around, as I was finishing up my coursework. I picked up tons of hours at Bob's Gym, often even picking up overtime. It was worth it. My reputation of being a hard-working, trustworthy and funny character at the gym, all three locations (at the time), was soon discovered. It was discovered so well that I eventually was given a promotion after rounds of interviews going into the New Year.

One thing I took great pride in aside from my philanthropy was my passion to dance still. TRL was not as prominent in my life, truth be told. However, the days of dancing and choreographing in my room as if I was live on the Video Music Awards stage for MTV were not long retired from.

I was recommended by a few people at the gym in Newburgh to start a Hip-Hop Dance Class. It was an early success, hitting max numbers and intriguing both members and non-members with the combination of dancing and cardio. This new project was something that was sentimental for me since I knew what it meant for me as a child to dance and feel good about myself, despite the highs and lows that life had.

In addition, I was also announced as the new Membership Advisor for Bob's Gym East, which used to be owned as Resultz Gym. The position and transition that came with it also made for an interesting time in my life. I was debating my moves, wanting to move to Memphis. It had been a dream job of mine for years to work for St. Jude's Children's Hospital as an event planner, or in public relations.

An old friend from college, Megan, had text me out of the blue. It was a pleasant surprise, as not too many of those came my way back then. I had planned on visiting her at the beginning of the year, later that next month. We caught up and reminisced about the past. A story about my 20th birthday party, the Mid-Summer Night's Dream theme one, came into play, too.

For now, I was a college graduate, working full-time, living with my parents and continuing to only hide a secret, but also continuing to live through it. I could not enjoy the little successes in my life. I began drinking heavily, as I even relapsed and used cocaine, snorting the day before my job at Bob's Gym came to an end.

Even my philanthropy efforts with USI, Riley Hospital for Children and Fanny Pak fell through due to sponsors backing out. I felt like a failure who was clingy to their final rope. Thoughts of negativity, departing from those most recent successes, forced my way down a shame spiral and out of control relapse for days.

When the smoke finally cleared, by the next week, I jumped and bolted at this occupational freedom to take a position as a Manager-in-Training with Abercrombie & Fitch in Memphis, Tennessee. This would be the first of a few moments where I developed the 'Bigger, Better . . . Now' complex I have grown into, oh so well.

<<< CHAPTER SIX >>>

MEMPHIS x 2 & CHICAGO

"Many of life's failures are people who did not realize how close they were to success when they gave up.

—Thomas Edison (1847-1931) American inventor and inventor

The theme for my Facebook status was '901 > 812.' That means that Memphis (901) is greater than Evansville (812). I was ready for a scenery change. I wanted to start from fresh, thinking all over again like I did in the eighth grade, moving to Naperville.

When you pick up and leave, regardless of the clarity in your side view mirror, there is a blind spot you do not always pick up in your rear view mirror. That was the case in regards to the demons and anxieties I had joyriding, or hitch hiking on my way to the next chapter in my life.

Memphis was a bigger city, with more attractions, bigger buildings, more jobs and people . . . overall, I saw it had more to offer me. The home of Southern

Hospitality, if you will, began to fuel a level of happiness, still, even today, becomes unmatched.

The position as MIT with Abercrombie & Fitch at the mall near Memphis, was at Germantown, TN. The mall is called Wolfchase Galleria. The position was going to be at the Collierville, TN store instead, a last minute switch. If you know me, and by now I think you, I hate surprises.

The distance was hard being further away from downtown Memphis where I was looking for apartments. For about two or three weeks, to save money, I roughed it. I lived in my car, minimal groceries, using Laundromats to wash clothes, gym guest passes to shower and gas station bathrooms to rinse and brush my teeth.

I was determined not to go back to Evansville or Newburgh. I wanted so bad to be on my own and not have to struggle. It became a waiting game to even hear about the official start date as neither location seemed to have a resolve for me. I moved back, heartbroken and disappointed. Those sentiments translated into depression and self-guilt, pity and shame. There was very little in my life I was happy or proud of.

There was a period of a couple of weeks where I ended up drinking at home while my parents were at work. I had no job yet until March. My mom got me a part-time job at Schnucks, a local grocery store in Newburgh where she had worked a few years previous. It was just after I also was offered a job at Beef 'O' Brady's down the street as a server.

My anxieties overtook me as I was starting two new jobs, one of which was in a new field. I did not make a huge announcement about me being back, so the majority of any friends or people I hung out with changed significantly.

I put on my best face forward as I was working again. The excitement of having a job, making money and being around people, often an audience at times to my personality projection, took over the negatives in my life.

When I would return home, or have a day off, those demons came to life and commandeered my life. I would avoid friends for normal hangouts and others birthdays, as I struggled with my own still. If it was a party with liquor, I would force my way over or find a friend to drive me, knowing I was already under the influence of booze.

My days of being a functional alcoholic and occasional cocaine user came back. The chemical dependency is what I had known for years, despite knowing better on my better days, though, they were few and far between.

Once I got adjusted to working both jobs, I set off to visit Megan at BSU, as she was still living there. So much had gone on in both of our lives since the last time we hung out. I had not even spoken to her ex,

Adam, who I was also close friends with at one point, as well.

It felt good to visit people, see places and explore my glory days of college. Those five years at BSU were the host to a type of catalyst in my life I had yet only begun to understand, much less acknowledge. It made things clearer to me once more, so I took a backseat to the cocaine use and opened up to people about the chemical dependency as it became a habit to turn to coworkers, friends and acquaintances about any detail in my life, except my brush with CSA.

Part of me felt like I was living a lie, but another part of me felt good just to feel like I was living, period. I was an open book, an animate personality and flamboyant comic throughout my days.

I hung around some friends I met at sand volleyball as the weather became warmer. I also started hanging out with my friends Kyle, who lived in the same neighborhood, and Josh, who also had worked at Bob's Gym. Aside from drinking with them, one of the activities we did together was spar, as in MMA. With my karate background and few rounds with friends in college, it was a nice distraction from my drama and gave me a chance to feel like a man.

I would feel like a little boy because I saw I had not grown up. My tendencies to be timid and shy around friends matched the same that I had with strangers. But to combat it, I would make jokes, becoming a center of attraction in the form of a clown or joker of some sorts.

I would make wise cracks, lacking filter or common sense at times to help fit in. Sometimes it would be at the expense of others, but more so myself in that case.

Self-deprecation is not the best form of flattery, much less, it is not the best method of coping with what I had and was going through. But, again, I knew no better, or at least neglected to take the better route to grace.

I made a few friends at Schnucks in Bonnie F., who I am still friends with today; Mark, who is not on my radar today; John S., Joe Mayse and Kyle A, who still are in my life, pretty close, too; Jacob, who is the same category as Mark. We would hang out, usually at Bonnie's apartment behind Schnucks.

Bonnie and Mark were the two best friends I had at Schnucks or in life at the time, as I became pretty close with James B., Ade L., Robin H., Tiffany D., Sarah Myers, Danielle M., Charlotte D. and Scot M. at Beef 'O' Brady's.

The regular work crew from both often mixed, whether it was a Corn Hole evening at the restaurant, or Trivia Night on a Tuesday evening at Ri-Ra's. Speaking of, that is where I met this girl named Mandie. She was short, cute, tan, blonde, pretty and had a contagious personality to match that golden smile.

We would talk and text each other often. She lived in Owensboro, so it was a commute for us to do anything. We tried to make sense of the chemistry between us, I perhaps was more interested in her, though.

Bonnie was the best wing-woman I could ask ever. She would plug my volleyball background and share that I looked good in spandex. That is a definite ice breaker with homer run capabilities, let me tell you.

The spring and early summer was all built up so I could make sense of my life and figure out what comes next. I still was looking at moving to Memphis. My birthday and a job offer all came together at once. What was originally planned as a group trip became a tag along interview and evening stay with Mark and I in Memphis.

We ended up celebrating my job offer at TGI Friday's. When I came back I had two weeks to pack, move, wrap up work and celebrate my birthday, that August 1st. The extra stress was far from anti-climactic. I would binge-drink beyond belief and even relapse, snorting twice that week before I moved.

I even walked out on Beef 'O' Brady's after finally putting a stop to the extra stress and negativity I went through with management. My friends understood, so I even stayed rolling silverware and doing side work, in hopes to not screw them over on a busy Friday night. I did not need passive aggressive, harassing and derogatory remarks to trigger anymore anxiety.

As tough as I could act or pretend to be, I am one of the most sensitive people I know because for years I held onto so much. The outpours were never channeled properly, as from here on out, work was not always a safe haven for me. Sometimes would play host or catalyst for an emotional and/or mental breakdown.

I did not want the previous self-conscious demons to strike me during a time in my life that I felt like it was my chance to be happy. I had failed. I moved a nervous wreck and my job in Memphis ended up being a hoax. It was a marketing scam that I did not catch on to until the first day.

I lasted a matter of thirty six hours in Memphis, before returning home. Memphis 2.0 was a bust, perhaps a more devastating bust to my psyche as it was sooner experienced and not much of a battle to make it work out.

*"I've missed more than 9000 shots in my career.
I've lost almost 300 games; 26 times, I've been
trusted to take the game winning shot and missed.
I've failed over and over and over again in my life.
And that is why I succeed."*

*—Michael Jordan (b. 1963) former professional
basketball player, entrepreneur and majority of the
Charlotte Bobcats*

I reverted to the liquor cabinet and soaked my despair with alcohol. I was able to get my job back at Schnucks, but did not care to go back to Beef 'O' Brady's. Again, I lost touch with some people within that week, alone. I wanted a fresh start with in some similar surroundings. It was like asking for gold in a silver mine, but you were still happy and accepting of anything grander than bronze.

Sonny N., who ran the volleyball leagues at Bob's Gym previously, now wound up running his programs at Metro Sports Center. I reached out to him and he brought me on board as a coach his first year at the new facility. So between both jobs, I worked and managed to make money, pay bills, spent some for personal enjoyment.

I became resentful of my past that my sharp enjoyment for humor and fun in life turned into salted bliss and a distain for happiness. I became bitter and felt like I deserved better, carrying a chip on my shoulder.

I neglected to go back to cocaine, but the drinking was still my exercise for tranquility. Though, often only temporary, just the quick fix and vice to sleep soundly without negativity and depression worked. There were continued random evenings I cried myself to sleep.

I worked through the fall, doing both jobs, leading up to the holidays when I began to unravel deeper and further than ever before. It was about the time Bonnie left Schnucks, I was quickly depressed and suicidal. Mass texts would go out to my high school and college friends saying I reached the end.

Kyle R., my roommate of two years, and one of my closest friends, who lives in New York, reached out to my father at his office. Kyle had informed him of the on-goings and mom intervened.

It got to the point where even my nasty and snippy nature towards some coworkers turned into cries for help and support. Jan S. and Laura V., my bosses at Schnucks, (as well as Annette S. & Ruthie P.) became a genuine audience to my tears and sniffles one weekday morning where I pleaded for a day off to be alone and just sleep, instead of putting on a happy face of work.

The shock of me turning down hours, after always wanting to work and pick up, surely came with red flags. They honored my request, Jan being the one I talked the most about it, as Laura walked away to tend to a customer need or phone call.

Jan offered her advice and perspective, recognizing where I was coming from. I never shared the part about me living with being molested as a kid, as I felt there was no place in the conversation with anyone for that factoid.

That night, I went out with some friends, needing to be around some familiar faces. I got so drunk, I passed out, puking in the bathroom at a friend's house. I missed my shift the next day as I overslept, remaining idle in the same woes. Jan assured me I was not fired, honest as she was. My anxiety was triggered as now I felt like I let down more people, my bosses and co-workers. I even became relentless with attitude and misperceived swagger at volleyball, often having an aggressive personality with a hint of cockiness, though faked or misdirected.

I was in rut, caught in a terrible cycle of pain and misery, with limited and temporarily forced happiness. I was settling for content but never achieving happiness. This became my new goal, but the means were unknown by me.

So I turned to another vice that is much healthier than drugs and alcohol, philanthropy. I called up Mrs. Rhonda Z. from the American Red Cross, where I did my community service from my DUI. I wanted to help put my degree to use and give my life something new, charity.

There was a Reverse Draw Benefit that they wanted to hold and I volunteered to raise donations, prizes to be raffled, promote the event and decorate it, too. People began to notice an uplifting movement in my aura. My smile felt natural, my energy was high, my ego was balanced and I felt well on my way to being truly happy.

The event went well. I even invited Mark's mother, Diana and Mark's twin brother, Karl. The three of us sat together as Mark was with his Dad that weekend. It was one of the most calming, relaxing, fulfilling evenings in my professional and personal life, nothing seemed to matter.

I felt blessed to be able to share it and use it as a launching pad to go forward. I wanted to work toward my dream job with St. Jude's Children Hospital again. Thus, that became my ultimate destination in my life for some time.

It was March, the next month. It was both Bonnie's and Mark's birthdays early on in the first week or so of the month. We did something fun for Bonnie's birthday, and then for Mark's as he became like a younger brother to me during all of this time, I threw him a hotel party. My friend Brian Enders, from BSU, came up from Bowling Green, KY to visit, too.

The party was a disaster as too many people showed up, Mark got my friend Brian lost in the midst of a liquor run. When I tried to resolve matters and bring attention to the maylay, I was confronted with an attack by Mark, when he told me 'You freak out about everything, sometimes I think you're better off going back to cocaine and OD'ing.'

He was drunk, but the words he formulated were like a dagger to me. I ended the party, which in return by the end of that weekend, I ended the friendship. The knife wound in my back still stung until I transitioned to me.

I still was not happy in Evansville, but hit a quick void of wanting 'Bigger, Better . . . Now!' I wanted to be in a big city, close to friends and family of my past and make up for some lost time I felt I allowed to slip away because of my anxiety, PTSD and insecurities.

I interviewed with Shoe Carnival in Elmhurst, Illinois, close to my Aunt Sue's place. Her and my cousin Ryan, have always been very inspiring and motivating people in my life. Their encouragement and support have made a difference in a number of occasions, including this one.

During this time, I also experienced a bit of a health scare with a mole on my neck which was diagnosed in Evansville that month as potentially cancerous. I never experienced a health scare like that since the one with my liver and the infections in college.

> "*You gain strength, courage, and confidence by every experience in which you really stop to look fear in the face. You are able to say to yourself, 'I lived through this horror. I can take the next thing that comes along.'*"
>
> *—Eleanor Roosevelt (1884-1962) Former First Lady and human rights activist.*

I went to see another doctor in the same week as my interview back up north near Chicago. The stress and anxiety of landing a job or not accompanied with that of not knowing if you may being sick, having cancer or just to find out you are in fact healthy, weighed heavily.

All in all, the week was a success, but an unplanned one. I was offered the job up north, but later looked elsewhere as Greg M. with WEVV-CBS Evansville offered me a job interview for an Account Executive position. I ended up being healthy, clear of skin cancer, as the mole was benign. This is also how I met a dear friend of mine, Tim B.

As fate would have it, I was not offered the position, solely on the fact that I had a DUI two years ago, as the position called for a clean driving record of three years. I rolled my rekindled confidence in being that close to the type of job I deserved into volleyball, as I did not retain my job at Schnuck's feeling like I wanted to pursue a different avenue.

By May, I found a part-time job at Abercombie & Fitch, in 2010. Once summer hit, my hours were stacked at Metro Sports Center, both coaching volleyball and working the Kids' Sports Camp as a counselor, then part-time as an Impact Associate with A & F at Eastland Mall.

I would play some sand volleyball early on in summer to stick with what I knew, playing to evade my issues. I met friends Paul S. and Megan P., among others. Today, these two are close friends of mine, as they played an important role in my life two years later.

In addition to volleyball at Metro and Wessleman's, I was asked to be a volunteer coach with Mrs. Lesley T. at Holy Rosary School, in Evansville, Indiana. The majority of the girls playing were athletes from Metro: Ellen T., Maddie McK., Victoria W., M.J. Schultz, Bridgette S., Olivia V., Ellie S and Emily A.

This was a nice break from my chaos to be able to help a bunch of girls, who I had for the most part, a history with and their families, from Metro. They loved the sport, though spent just as much time as me being goofy at practices. They improved drastically that year compared to the year before. They were so much fun to be around, as those Tuesday, Thursday practices were my favorite days on my calendar or planner.

Working the summer camps I knew was temporary, I also knew that I needed a regular source of income during the fall, so I took an interview across the street with Tri-State Athletic Club as a Membership Sales Rep.

In addition to the Sales Rep position, I took on event planning, public relations and even worked on bringing my Hip-Hop Dance Class to life. Our team and work force became pretty close. April F. and Stacey H. were hired a week or two after me, as we became a three person team.

Tom M. was our boss. He is a father, husband, with a lovely family, one that I admire. Tom was successful, fashionable, athletic and in shape. I looked up to that, things I did not have but wanted. My boss became an inspiration to my hard work, as to have something for myself to show for it.

I struggled to meet membership sales quota, find regularity in my nerves being there, as I felt an enormous level of pressure. I was filling a role of woman, Eileen, who was very successful at her job, and to please my boss Tom, who I held on a pedestal. The 'Bigger, Better . . . Now!' concept in my life became overdone.

It became a well-documented and well refined skill of mine to balance and maintain multiple jobs during any given season(s). Eventually, due to conflict of interest at TSAC, I had to step down from Metro Sports Center in all functions. I still worked at A & F, though my direct supervisor, Tiffany, who was referred to as moody, shifty and pretentious, stuck me on her apparent hit list and my hours were diminished and I was written up for a few offenses that never happened, much less, were piled up 'all of a sudden.'

This happened as I was prepared to step down from TSAC, wanting to find something new. My dad even took me to lunch. I thought, wow this might be a chance to talk to him about what really has been going on. I balked at another opportunity to open up to my own father. That alone, made me feel down about myself and created a sense of rekindled disappointed around the situation.

I gained one of my closest friends from this job at TSAC, Mrs. Deirdre H. She has always been there for me as she is the type of loving, devoted wife and mother of a gorgeous family that you can't help but do the same for.

I accepted a paid internship in town, right across from the mall at Health Resources, Inc. Becky Z., one of the mothers from Metro Volleyball was so kind as to offer me the job. I interviewed and was offered formally, becoming an intern and picking up extra hours in the mailroom.

There I met Whitney U., The Wilson Girls', other employees, including Lindsay L., my supervisor. She was tall, slender, brunette, with an auburn tint . . . what the hell would I know, I can't see red, but I knew she was not a blonde. I loved her eyes, I loved smile . . . I enjoyed her, more to come.

I played one last day of sand volleyball outside before the weather got colder down at Wessleman's park. I was talking to a friend out in Los Angeles, CA. My ambitions to move to Memphis, TN switched gears as I declared an old endeavor to move west. LA would become my new playground, I was determined of that. The next year, or less, proved to be my crowning achievement towards happiness and peace.

<<< CHAPTER SEVEN >>>

FROM MEMPHIS 3.0 TO LOS ANGELES BEGINS

"Action may not always bring happiness . . .
but there is no happiness without action."

—Benjamin Disraeli (1804-1881) Former British
Prime Minister

I came into one of the Holy Rosary volleyball practices, ready to share the news that I was aiming to move to Los Angeles, CA and make the most of my changes. I was prepared to settle with A & F as a mere part-time, part-time job. HRI was the focus of my work, gaining 30-40 hours a week. Green River Road was the sight for both jobs, separated only by traffic, a median and a Taco Bell.

I worked as much as I could not only for the money, but the experience. I felt validated in my hours and responsibilities; I felt appreciated and respected by most co-workers and bosses, as I was not gaining such notoriety from home or with friends.

Well, that is not completely true . . . There was one common compliment that became the saving grace for it all when it came to my confidence: 'You are one of the hardest working people I know.'

Such a bold claim for my character, even though, half of my rationale and logic was to bury my feelings and issues with the hours upon hours I would work. Sometimes, I even over did it. Nonetheless, if there is one thing that I have probably established thus far about me is that I am relentless and that I am a rebounder. I am like the Dennis Rodman or Dwight Howard of life, that's how many times I feel like I have rebounded.

By Halloween, I earned a promotion at Abercrombie & Fitch, becoming a Manager in Training, then assistant manager at Hollister (same company), in addition to my internship at HRI. I balanced both well, at first. Then, it all caught up to me.

I officially filed my paperwork to apply for graduation after transcript issues from USI, over the course of two years. Some people should not be in clerical work, let me tell you. However, fate prevailed and I received my letter stating that I would graduate in December. Going into November, I wanted to better myself. I changed the way I did some things, including becoming a vegetarian.

The holidays were nuts, as I was working on this move to California. I had invited Megan to move out with me, since we were still really close friends. I reached out to everyone I knew that lived out there on Facebook.

For three months, I lasted out, no longer eating meat (perhaps once a week, as a predetermined cheat). That is impressive since I indulge in McDonald's Dollar Menu quite often. Three months . . . that is a whole trimester of being a vegetarian. I would relapse and eat meat in late January.

I was working close with my boss Devin M, co-assistant manager Maggie W. and full-time stock Ashley M. I knew about 25% of the employees already through friends of mine or my brothers and sister. It may not have been the best situation given the company has a strict fraternization policy. Funny how not following it set up one the best worst situations of my life, which we will get to shortly.

By December, I think it was the 15th or 17th, I had the biggest melt down. I even walked out at Hollister, though it only lasted twenty five minutes. Kayla P., our District Manager, called me up and wanted to make sure that I was ok. She and I always got along and we did respect each other for the work we did. She went up to bat for me a lot, more than Devin, my store manager, had done.

There was a world of drama around my store manager that contributed to some of my anxiety. It even put Maggie and Ashley against me and one another at times. I quote Yolanda Foster when she says 'There's nothing less classy than a drunk woman.'

The holidays were stressful, given that I was in retail. I remember Christmas and New Years were two holidays I wanted to avoid and I looked forward to the spring when I planned on moving to Los Angeles. I had pushed the date back a few times because of finances, living arrangements and job search issues.

By the end of January though, the unexpected happened. A guy by the name of Kerr, (this was not his real name, but is kept anonymous for reasons to be shared later) applied at Hollister. He came in during Maggie's shift and met Christine, another employee, who I am still also friends with. I had learned he was crushing on her and wanted the job. He interviewed well, along with another guy named Jesse. Jesse had known my sister from working at Shoe Carnival, across the street.

They both got the job, but only Kerr lasted . . . well, past the first two weeks. Jesse was a no call, no show. Kerr and I became close. We hung out, played volleyball, went lifting, drank and smoked together. In such a short time, he became like a younger brother to me.

After Maggie stepped down from Hollister, we all planned a going away party for her. Kerr and I got drunk and high that evening. The dinner for everyone was at Olive Garden, and then went bowling at Arc Lanes. The night cap was supposed to be an after party at Drury Inn, but only Kerr and another new hire, Ryan D. made it there. Ryan passed out drunk a little early. Kerr and I stayed up in the suite talking and shooting the shit with each other.

We only knew each other for three weeks, as he opened up about his home life, background and childhood.

Maybe it was the liquor, as a flashback of that weekend at Purdue struck my conscious of when I talked to Kyle R. and Jack B. I took the opportunity as I often neglected to ignore it or take a pass on it.

I told Kerr about my eleventh birthday. There was full detail provided, without the emotional outpour of crying, shriveling or stammering that used to come with it. I shared that I was looking into taking advantage of our Employee Assistance Program at Hollister and utilize the free counseling for full-time management with the company.

Kerr was the most supportive figure in my life, at that time. He understood my insecurities, struggles and anxiety. The post-traumatic stress disorder symptoms and effects were off the radar between the anxiety and tension caused by balancing two jobs, planning my move to Los Angeles, finding myself in my career and wanting to pursue my Master's Degree in Public Relations.

I had already had my first counseling session, the day after I shared with my mother about my 11th birthday. It came with that emotional outpour that lacked during the time I shared with Kerr. The setting was not an after party for this one, as I called my mom on her cell from my car in the parking lot of a Wal-Mart.

Two weeks later, I resigned from Hollister. I went on a Spring Break trip with some of the girls from Hollister, Kerr tagged along. He and I only went down for the two or three days. I needed an escape, to do something for me. The girls were fun, though the age difference did provide some drama. However, the whole time I was also thinking about how being by the beach in Panama City, Florida for Spring Break was close to that of Los Angeles, CA.

That week after PCB, I had inquired about my Masters in Public Relations again. I felt like the timing was right. I wanted to attend the University of Memphis Online. Or, now, knowing that my internship with Lightning Bolt—USA and my lease was just for the thirteen weeks of summer, I found about the University of Northern Iowa from an advisor. This was where Kerr was transferring.

During this time, I met up with a friend, Shelley W., one of the mothers from Metro Volleyball. She and I are still great friends to do this day. We ate at a pizza place, Kippley's, and caught up. The stress of my upcoming transition and exploring of my recovery from CSA was put on the table.

Shelley is a friend I felt comfortable being boldly honest with. I shared that I felt like I was rushing my decision to move to LA and then to Iowa after. I admitted to her my nerves of trusting my future roommate Kerr and some holes in his stories and stuff. I told her that I was in between running away from my problems or sprinting too fast to solve them.

That dinner did wonders for me as I began opening up to more familiar and friendly faces of my past and present. Gut instincts prevail and just sharing a piece, or in my case, pieces of yourself help put the puzzle together. I rarely do puzzles alone because I admit I do need help. Growing up, I could not put those words together because of fear, anxiety, but as well as some pride and self-absorbed tendencies to do it all and want it all for myself. I competed with myself too often.

Yes, curiosity struck me and after the trip, the way it went down, I felt comfortable possibly being his roommate up there if he felt cool with it because it would save me a boat load for in-state tuition. I remember telling both Maggie and Christine first, because I did not want Kerr to feel like I was invading him and his life to make mine play out. I also would never chase a friend across the country as my career has always been a dominant fixation in my planning.

Kerr's response to my inquisition was 'Yes, I told you it was cheap to go there!' So, I pursued it and was planning on moving to Iowa in early August, after my birthday. That was another level of stress itself, planning a move after a move. Not only that, but I also had to worry about my birthday. I felt like I had to celebrate it and make a big deal of it given my progress in therapy and tackling many of the demons stemming from my eleventh birthday.

Now, I found myself desperate for a lot of things. Perfection was the biggest, but I knew what I wanted was to be happy, let down my guard and to feel confident in whom I am. The past mistakes and blunders made sense in therapy. I was open about seeing a counselor and told people why. Sharing with friends about me being sexually molested on my eleventh birthday felt like the beginning steps of cleansing myself. Though it felt overdue, it still felt magical.

Before it closed up in Evansville, Sonny and I went to Borders and hung out. We were catching up about my move and my future. He has always been very honest, straight-forward and most certainly genuine in caring about my best interest. He shared with me how he felt like I may be rushing everything and putting a lot of trust into friends because I did not quite have that trust in myself.

Sonny may have hit the nail on the head. I know who he was referring to. Even more than that, Sonny knows we both admit that I am a difficult person to get along with because I placed such an emphasis on trust, loyalty and honesty with friends, especially male friends. Sonny has never failed or let me down in that category; very few can say that.

I spent the whole spring gearing up for the biggest shift of my life. Before the initial one, I switched jobs and started serving at Red Robin. I met new friends, Taylor H., Devin V., Seth K., Ally B., and more. I got the job from Heather F., who I knew from summer camps at Metro. I used to babysit her son Jayden, too.

The stress built up between the internship, serving at Red Robin, planning the move to L.A. and my therapy. April was when I hit a breaking point. A productive and really deep day of therapy contributed to an evening where I wrote a note a Facebook. It was my declaration of freedom and a release of self-inflicted persecution from being a victim and survivor of Child Sexual Abuse.

Tuesday, April 5th, 2011,

Today is another gorgeous day outside. The sun is out, the air is fresh and there is a lot to be happy about. The last few months have been no different than the rest of my life: a rollercoaster! I have been through the highs & lows and ups & downs more times than I even desire to count.

One of the biggest obstacles and tragic moments in my life, I have finally stopped brushing under the carpet and pretending like it never bothered or hurt me. I was sexually molested on my 11th Birthday and for three years never told anyone, except for one teacher. I didn't tell another person until I went away to college. Just two months ago, I had told probably the 11th or 12th person, life time.

That person (Thank You, you know who you are!) I told that day was the first time I took the next step: asking how to tell my parents, and how to approach therapy. For 14 years I pretended like it never happened and then feeling guilty for doing something wrong at the same time. I allowed myself to grow weaker; my self-concept diminished, my anxiety developed and intensified, and I continually shut people down, or out. I was harming myself just as much as the man who took from me something I'll never get back on my 11th Birthday.

I have spent the last 8 or more years talking myself out of happiness, cutting friends, relationships, jobs, because I didn't feel worthy of them. I would short change myself and tell myself I was ugly, too skinny, too fat, too pale, too flamboyant, too emotional, too stuck up: too much of who I wasn't!

In less than 7 weeks, I am about to take those steps forward towards my career, my happiness, my life back. I've spent the last month with a therapist talking about everything, opened up to new and old friends along the way, as well. I've even begun writing a book, 'Ankle Deep,' sharing my life and the tragedy that beset me 14 years ago.

I only let myself go 'Ankle Deep' into things: relationships, friendships, jobs, anything new, etc. That me is dead and gone. I have reasons to celebrate and not worry . . . or at least not as much as I do hah! I would doubt myself and the friendships, relationship Ive had and feel I wasn't even worthy of them. I thought for years because one prick who molested me had done me so wrong, anyone else could or would. Those negative thoughts and emotions have taken its toll on me and even others; that is not fair to do or settle with.

The friends I have are the greatest in the world, because of each and every one of them I have been able to get my life back on track, get to where I know I belong and am no longer settling for what is good at the time. I am 25, and this is the year 2011; I'm ready to do me! I don't feel like being molested and having my life in terms of trust, confidence, faith in anyone and everything being crippled is going to prevent me from doing what I want in my life!

Thank you to all of my friends, family, coworkers, bosses, and acquaintances that have helped me hold my head where it should be, and that is up high! If there ever were days were I was an asshole, or stressed the f*** out to where I got annoying or hurtful, I am sorry. I won't throw into the 'I have post-traumatic anxiety & depression' syndrome from being molested bucket . . . but I know those apologies are necessary, old and new!

You never know when you need one of those days to look at something so powerful to keep you on track in life. This time I am not cutting myself short and throwing it away! I love my life, I love my family, my friends and everyone Ive ever gotten to reach out to, or that has reached out to me.

To everyone tagged, thank you for reading and for helping me become a better me! Please comment and write your words of support, friendship, love, etc. It would mean the world for me to see everyone's reflection . . .

[Please don't take offense, if I didn't tag you . . . I spent an hour on this note in the middle of one of the best workouts I've had in two weeks lolz!] Again, I love my friends, my family and the life I'm not only living now . . . but I am about to embark on in the future . . . My future!

Colton Kyle likes this.

Stephanie Dean West This brought me joy to read, Scott. Congratulations on your new, non-self-torturing life. You're awesome and you do have so many people who care about you
April 5, 2011 at 6:99pm · Like

Melissa Ball Greer WOW! Amazing through all time I have known you its so nice to see you be "YOU" think for yourself and to have your own opinion is wonderful. I am so happy for you overcoming this traumatic experience in your life. Thank you for being a wonderful friend...See More
April 5, 2011 at 7:10pm · Like

Hilary Marie Scott im so happy for you! Im glad your on the highway to happiness!! Everyone deserves that! Keep it up man!!!! See ya in may
April 5, 2011 at 7:21pm · Like

Lauj Cameron I am so proud of you for taking the next step in life! You mean the world to me! Just keep on looking up and forward!
April 6, 2011 at 6:35am · Like

Deirdre Wilson Hartman Thank you for being a awesome part of MY life!!! !!!!
April 6, 2011 at 5:16pm · Like

April Chappelle Scott, I love you, and I love being your friend. I wish you nothing but the best for your future. I'm glad you are being able to see yourself the way everybody else sees you. You are the amazing Scott Thomas Sieg!
April 7, 2011 at 1:03pm · Like

Colton Kyle Love ya man good luck with everything ahead of you
April 10, 2011 at 8:26pm via mobile · Like

James Webb Scott love u man u have been a true friend to me and are a great person!!!...we had the best times in undergrad!!!
April 11, 2011 at 7:33pm · Like

Kyle Ramsy We all have those negative feelings and emotions and its how you deal with them that defines us as a person. I am so glad to hear that you have a new outlook in life. Remember as long as you continue to be the great person/friend as you are and been, y...See More
April 17, 2011 at 4:54pm · Like

_____

I was so proud of my note on Facebook that by the time my last therapy session with Dr. Buxton, I invited Kerr to be there as a witness for another letter to renounce my status as a victim to pledge my new found notoriety as a survivor of CSA.

The three days I flew out to Los Angeles were the Wednesday night thru Friday night in California. I would get back that Saturday morning and work a double at Red Robin. But that is what I needed to do to make this arrangement happen.

I stayed with my friend Charlie W. and his roommate Michael K. They both were the best of hosts, people with manners, class and genuine friendship. They had genuine support for my happiness and me being in Los Angeles. I wound up playing volleyball at the YMCA in Westchester and met some nice people, who very welcoming. I hit the freeway and Interstates with ease, rarely getting lost or having any sort of panic attack. I even forgot to take my medication while out there because I did not need. I hit the beach, got tan. I came back dark, people were jealous. I basked in my new complexion.

At this point, along with the therapy, I was on my second month with my prescription of Prestiq. My anxiety medication worked, but the level of stress I possessed through therapy, relocating and working two jobs still triggered some anxiety attacks. Taylor, my coworker at Red Robin, could relate, but my attacks (both of us admit) mine are worse.

That weekend I was so stressed and overwhelmed. I spent a number of nights blowing up peoples' phones, mass texting, calling and Facebooking people to have someone to talk or catch up with. The more social I felt, the less alone I thought I would feel. Sometimes, it made it worse.

It was in the middle of the week during mid-May that I had my final counseling session with Dr. Buxton. That day was extremely emotional, both good and bad, but raw nonetheless. I felt as if I just ran a marathon but only completed it using my heart and my mind. I was exhausted from that evening.

The dinner I planned on having at Red Robin with Kerr was cancelled last minute because of an arrangement that was supposedly sprung on him last minute. This tended to be theme throughout the 'friendship.' I own up to putting extra emphasis on people and friends, especially in holding their word. In fact, I am guilty of letting people down or cancelling on plans. However, a level of ownership needs to follow. I am big on manners, others are . . . well, not.

The same situation would arise the night before I was supposed to drive to California. I was going to drive up to his place in Iowa and then to Denver, CO, then to Las Vegas, NV and then a short drive to Los Angeles, all by myself now. Something came up, though perhaps legit, the presentation and timing sucked. But I made due.

My time in Los Angeles was rich. I quote my friend Lori R. back from Evansville and Newburgh, Indiana when she says 'If you can make it in Los Angeles, you can make it anywhere.'

<<< CHAPTER EIGHT >>>

FROM L.A. TO 'IOWA' A LOT OF PEOPLE SOME THANKS

"Criticism may not be agreeable but it is necessary. It fulfills the same functions as pain in the body. It calls attention to an unhealthy state of things."

—Winston Churchill (1874-1965) Politician, statesman and former British Prime Minister

And I did. I balanced my internship with Lightning Bolt—USA, transferring out to Red Robin in Northridge as a server, finding work with Adidas in Santa Monica on 3rd Street Promenade and making friends, memories and the most of my new life.

This new life was filled with writing my book, finding me, testing who I am and what I am capable of, pushing the envelope and developing myself into the man I wanted and longed to be: Confident, proud, outgoing, social, responsible, stable and myself.

I was not hiding behind a celebrity picture on my Facebook. I was not pretending to be someone I was not. Instead I was working on finding out who I could be, naturally. The drive to Los Angeles was lonely as I am not a fan of having time to myself. During a three and a half day, 30-some hour road trip, you might end up getting sick of you.

To keep occupied, I blared *N'Sync, Justin Timberlake, Timbaland and Britney Spears CD's like a damn fool. I also continued this little habit of pretending to be interviewed by Jay Leno, Ryan Seacrest or Barbara Walters. It could be Letterman, Larry King, Chelsea Lately or any other big-time journalist, but that was my way of talking to God, the few times I sought out to.

My relationship with God was small, though I still considered myself an atheist. I also took my stance on trying to find Faith as declaring myself a 'religious free agent.' These talks or faux interviews were my way of decreasing the stress, calming my nerves and refocusing my drive. It was my aspiration to one day be famous, of course. Many people have that yearning to be loved, famous and respected.

It has been a personal dream of mine to be on the cover of *GQ, Forbes* and *Details*. I also wanted to host 'Saturday Night Live,' have my book published and become a New York Bestseller. Hell, I considered trying out to be a backup dancer and hoping I hit the hook-up lottery like K-Fed and Chris Judd did with Britney Spears and Jennifer Lopez, respectively. Or my second method would be to apply as a pool boy for one of the Real Housewives of Beverly Hills, now that my 'Ankle-Deep' restriction was self-lifted and removed.

That is correct people. I swam in the Pacific Ocean at Venice Beach. I let loose the worries I brought cross-country with me in the ocean water. I felt cleansed. I would try it in the beach waters of Manhattan Beach, Hermosa Beach and Redondo Beach.

That summer, my roommates were: Katie P., Denise K., Suzie, Rasheed, and Phil C. We all got a long, but saw little of each other. I got along better with the girls, but made friends with some locals and neighbors like Bryan P. and Pat S.

I made quick friends with the people at Red Robin. They embraced my efforts, both personally and professionally. Erin F., Jordan S., Ashlee M & Matt B., Kaylie M., Kristi W., Julie & Ryan B., Shane J., Tabitha, Sarah, Marie, Eddie, Connie (we even had a host named Michael Jackson, too) and my managers Spike, Fonzie, Oscar, Amanda, Sal & Astyn, they all looked out for me, knowing I was from Indiana, on my own, out and about trying to find myself in this thirteen week window.

The same blessed situation happened at Adidas. I was introduced and embraced by a family of peers, coworkers and new friends. Amira A., Jimmy, Mark, Stephanie, Ashley and Ambrey, Faith, Laura, Robert, Veronica, Gerson, Josh, Felipe, Carter, Giovanni, Melly and so many more.

Both work staffs understood my anxiety and I was open about my book and wanting to start my life fresh with my new swag. The writing was coming along and I met a girl out there that sparked a new side to me: Mrs. Christine W.

I randomly saw her at Art Walk in July and approached her, giving her my number and asking her out. I would cook for her and we hung out. We still talk and text even today, as we are positively supportive and help influence each other's path.

The summer dragged at times, then flew by at others. The birthday weekend was the most stressful. Kerr was flying in and upon waiting for his flight to land, his girlfriend Megan started an argument with me about her boyfriend drinking and was not please when I told her that 'if she could not reach Kerr tomorrow night between 6-8p her time, it was because we were out to dinner with a big group for my birthday.' The little girl, who was a minor, turned it around to say I was telling her when she could and couldn't reach her boyfriend.

In addition to the stress of moving to Iowa from Los Angeles, saying my farewells, closing one chapter and opening another to find myself further in Iowa, she stirred the pot and this was the first log on the Jenga friendship to make the tower falter.

I became super close with KC, Brittany C. & Kyle H., Bryant G., Andre P. & Lauren S., Ryan S., Jessie P., Austin Z. and Sarah R., Jennica R., Reese G. and a few others within this group. I had played sand volleyball and beer pong with most of them the first night in town. I drove up to Cedar Falls from Kerr's house after staying with his family for a little more than a week. His parents were humble hosts, especially his mother, but his girlfriend creeped me out (I know that sounds harsh and rude to say, however, the opinion was shared and recognized by future neighbors and friends of mine). I knew it was best to give them all a night without me.

I found myself getting deeply involved at the Family YMCA of Black Hawk County, enjoying the real reasons why I moved to Iowa in the first place. Drama is dangerous because it fuels ambition for me. I will not start it but I get involved when I feel like I can better the situation. After my job and internship at the YMCA, meeting a new group of incredible friends and changing my life for the better because my health hit another scare, I decided to move on.

The friendship ended between Kerr and I tried to avoid his clingy girlfriend who was over almost every day and every night. I am the type of person where if I do not want you around, I am straight forward and try to be polite about it. Delicacy was best suited for this level of crazy and I struggled to handle my own situations.

It got ugly with the living situation, as I even contributed to an investigation with Black Hawk County Drug Task Force in regards to my former friend. I doubt if the friendship was ever really genuine, or if it was a smoke screen for someone who took advantage of my vulnerability. I learned the answer to this that October.

One night, while entertaining friends that I have made within the apartment complex, I asked his girlfriend to leave. I told her that she can return to her own dorm until her boyfriend came home. Things were at an all-time intensity between us as she found out through listening in on a conversation over the phone I had in my room, her boyfriend cheated on her in PCB. He did not even own up to the whole truth and threw me under the bus shortly after Labor Day weekend.

I think he found it fitting to tell me off and through his bedroom door, as well as mine, he told me that I deserved what happened to me on my eleventh birthday. I was stunned, devastated. I instantly text my friend Austin Z. and my other friend Garrett. Garrett did not come to my defense and favored a drunk-party before our friendship. Austin had my back and to this day still does. My group of friends was there for me. The situation took its toll on me.

The old me may have let a comment like that lower me, knocking me off my path. I even shared the first part of my book with Kerr and I was stabbed in the back so deep it hit my heart. Statistics show that a common symptom or effect of Child Sexual Abuse is that victims and survivors can face being victimized or attacked verbally in regards to their own incident. My darkest memory and terror of my life was used a stone to be thrown at me.

I quickly worked on switching living arrangements and moved in with a friend from work at the YMCA, Justin S. Shortly after, I left the YMCA and took on two jobs, one with Life-Line Resources doing Behavioral Health Intervention Services and the second, with Hinduja Global Services as a customer service representative over the phone lines for AT&T Lifeline Plan.

Both jobs had 'life-line' in the title or description. I think it was just as symbolic as it was ironic. My new roommates Justin and my friend Alex M., who moved up from Evansville, IN, had my back and supported me celebrating the New Year, 2012, finishing up this book.

The friends I met from the original apartment, living situation, still hung out with me. We would not do our weekly Poker Nights anymore, or get drunk during the RHOBH on a Wednesday afternoon around noon. I lost a fake friend and gained twenty. I felt like the cruise ship trying to take off for sea but finally remember to lift the anchor up. I had no one or nothing holding me back.

The holidays were celebrated with family. Thanksgiving with my Aunt Sue, cousin Ryan and my grandmother (Nana). I moved before Christmas into that house with Justin and Alex, then meeting neighbors and more friends like Nick H. & Alyx S., Jesse T., Brian T., Sadie R., Natalie F., Lauren D. and more.

I did not want my journey to end with the book. After all my new found success and spiritual empowerment for not settling in my life, nor accepting any level of indecency from people, friends, coworkers, family or past figures in my life, gave me the drive I have today. I decided to use my experience with multiple non-profit organizations, my college degree in advertising and work in public relations to start my own charity.

I began my search for publishers sending my half manuscript with a marketing plan. I received a lot of feedback, mainly responses of declining interest and warm wishes, until the third yes, Author House Publishing, called me, one day in Feb. I landed a self-publishing deal and began working on my charity, The Shades 4 U Foundation.

At the end of any dark, dreary storm, lies a cloud with silver lining. The sun comes through and shines on the world's beautiful creatures. It provides life, a light to bestow its significance and appeal. My storm is behind me and the sun is pouring in on my life.

"A day without laughter is a day wasted."

—Charlie Chaplin (1889-1977) Singer, actor and performer.

Far different than the one that took place in 1996 my birthday was finally special to me for my 27th. I was not getting overly intoxicated on a separate date to avoid recognizing another year of life. Nor was I forcing myself to celebrate it with a motley crew of familiars, new roommates or fake friends pretending to be supportive. My surroundings were much more meaningful than an empty apartment room before move out day in LA like it was the year before.

I was with friends, hosting a double at Old Chicago, the restaurant where I work and love. On my lunch break I even brought in cupcakes to Metro Sports Center to share because I love kids. I look forward to the day I get to be a loving, dedicated and respectable father and husband to my own family. I do not have the fears and anxieties about that either, as I would see my own friends and family members developing theirs.

It was a dinner with cocktails (for those who are of age) at Old Chicago and I loved it. Kaylee M., one of the servers who trained me, got promoted along with me and someone I call a dear friend, as well as another server, Susan S., also a loving and caring individual, were taking care of our group. We took up about 20-30 seats.

There were no avoidances, anxieties or flashbacks. It felt surreal to live a 'normal' day on August 1st. Maybe that is the way this chapter or book should end, but only to begin the next one. I learned to let go of the past. Yes, it is still a part of me, but it does not define me. What I do today, in the now, defines me.

I forgave the man who molested me. I do not forget about it or him, but I choose not to dwell on the negatives it brought me. The same applies in regards to every failed relationship: intimate, professional, personal or romantic. This includes the former roommate who victimized me with the ill-fated and ill-willed comment that I deserved it. Today, I choose to give him and his girlfriend benefit of the doubt that they knew I would do better than what I was, rising about my past just as much as theirs. So thank you for that knife in the back, because now I have one to cut my celebration cake with!

Today, I have a lot to celebrate and eat cake for. It gives me great solace to share with friends, family, coworkers and strangers alike about being a victim and more so, a survivor of Child Sexual Abuse. My family knows about my past, the pain and perseverance in addition to the progress and my prevalence (that is a lot of P's to be aware of).

I live in Newburgh, Indiana, back at home with my parents as of publishing this book, writing my next and developing my charity. I work at Metro Sports Center as a volleyball coach and trainer, as well as a counselor for field trips, day care and Birthday Parties. I also switched from working as a server at Red Robin a second time in Evansville to serving, hosting and being a Certified Trainer at Old Chicago Restaurant. Both work environments have played host to me as great additional family-like support and love. I am spoiled at and by both!

I am 27 at the time of publishing this. 'Bigger, Better . . . Now!' picks up from my 27th Birthday, a happy time, for once. I reflect on putting together the 'Ankle-Deep' Tour, my charity (The Shades 4 U Foundation), dating, finding myself religiously, personally, spiritually, physically (health conscious) and balancing my Masters and not being a total nut-job.

The Shades 4 U Foundation is in its incubation period and I am currently working on creating it from the ground up. Through this book, the early stages of development for my own non-profit, charitable organization, the creation of my own book and PR tour in April 2013 (National Awareness Month for Child Sexual Abuse) and the continuing journey of my life as a survivor and hopeful guide to others, I am no longer 'Ankle-Deep' and I am on to 'Bigger, Better . . . Now!'

"Nothing gives an author so much pleasure as to find his works respectfully quoted by other learned authors."

—Benjamin Franklin (1706-1790, One of the Founding Fathers of the United States

<<< CHAPTER NINE >>>

MY SELF-HELP GUIDE TO SURVIVORS OF CSA

1. Let It Go!
2. Don't Brace Yourself, Embrace Yourself
3. Set Sail Without an Anchor
4. Take Everything In and . . . Breathe

1. 'Let It Go!'

I will be the first one to admit that I am the biggest grudge holder. I do not necessarily hold on to things long, but I hold them hard. It is hard to forgive early on for me because I deal better with resentment from pain rather than resenting the pain itself.

Emotional instability is not an attractive quality to have as a leader or role model; two things that I aspire to me through my philanthropy work with my charity and books.

Yes, I have forgiven the person who had sexually molested me on my eleventh birthday. It was the best decision in my life. That is why I look forward to eventually forgiving the former friend who told me that I deserved it (See, I told you that I, too, struggle to 'Let It Go!' sometimes).

The point is, when you 'Let It Go!,' you not only move on, but you move forward. In forgiving my attacker, I allowed myself to not only grow but to also heal. I do not view myself as a victim. I no longer victimized myself with the shame, guilt, embarrassment or the lack of self-confidence or self-worth.

After a certain amount of time, you discover that you are now attacking yourself. I am not saying that being molested all of a sudden no longer stops becoming a big deal or that it instantly will delete itself in a sort of unplanned epiphany. It begins with you and you have to 'Let It Go!'

You can't change the past, you can only live in the present to establish a better future. I used to be 'Ankle-Deep' in a lot of areas: trust, confidence, relationships and more. Now, because I 'Let It Go!,' I am 'Bigger, Better . . . Now!,' which is also the title of my second book, a follow up to Ankle-Deep.

Because I 'Let It Go!' I was able to turn around my situation and build a career out of helping others out the predicament I was in. I get to bring a voice and face to the little boy I used to be, struggling to identify with anyone, feeling alone.

It is such a fulfilling opportunity to write about my life: past, present and future. I 'Let It Go!' and I do not regret it. I am wishful that it happened sooner. However, regardless of my religious status, I have always believed that everything happens for a reason.

There are mere coincidences from time to time, but in my life, it is a blueprint. The design may seem all sorts of sporadic and out of sync. Perhaps by design itself, nonetheless, everything has come together for me in the end. I am forever grateful for all the good in my life because I remember when it used to be worse. That is why you simply just need to 'Let It Go!'

2. Don't Brace Yourself, Embrace Yourself.

I am the world's biggest planner. My follow through is not always on point. I will own up to that, myself. I tend to map things out, often writing my day, week or month out for work, jobs, my charity, working out, or even did the same when I was in college.

It is a nasty little habit of mine to detail my life, living it to a clipboard and outline way too often. 'Don't Brace Yourself, Embrace Yourself.'

Sometimes, you just can't account for every little detail, scenario or interference. It leaves you the choice of either handling it like a grown *ss adult, or you can do what I have built a reputation of doing and that is freak out, having a classic anxiety attack over something potentially miniscule.

Like I said, I am big on honesty. I have freaked out because we have run out of two beers at a restaurant and I did not know about that ahead of time. I mean, this was a Code Red meltdown.

I put myself in stressful situations, stock piling on jobs, commitments and other projects to fill a void in my life. But I also do it because I try to brace myself for the worst or unknown financial or professionally.

You can't live life going through the motions of constantly preparing for the 'what if's.' Where is the fun in that? 'Don't Brace Yourself, Embrace Yourself.' Recognize who you are by recognizing who you are not, sometimes.

It is ok to be human. I have accepted that after about two and a half decades of pulsing failures and success stories. It is not worth the stress, anxiety or freaking out, though the meltdowns in my case may be comical from the outside looking in.

I can't tell you enough how important it is to have flexibility. Maybe it is my karate and gymnastics background that allows me to more flexible now. Nevertheless, you can't be a Debbie Downer, a worry-wart, or a spaz about sh*t.

Look at yourself in the mirror. At one point, it was one of the hardest things for me to do, even during my cocaine addiction (sorry for the inappropriate joke, I am full of them this year). The blemishes you see are on the mirror itself. There are finger prints, from you and others, smudges and sometimes cracks. Though, those are harder to fix.

Why brace yourself, for the you that you are, when you should embrace it instead? We are each a gift to the world for the gifts we have to offer. Every person has a purpose. The man who molested me has one, even outside of fueling my recovery and this book/charity. Same goes for the prick who told me I deserved it. I embraced the negatives with the positives, in due time.

'. . . Embrace Yourself' as you have so much to offer outside of any tragedy, incident or predicament that you may feel labels you or holds you back. For a while, I thought I was permanently scarred from being molested, even growing up. I viewed myself as an outcast because I myself, thought I was alone and that people looked down on me and others for being victims of CSA.

The worst thing you can do is assume. It is worse when assume things about you for other people. Sometimes, you just have to say f*ck it. 'Don't Brace Yourself, Embrace Yourself!'

3. Set Sail Without an Anchor

If you want something bad enough you have to have Faith that you will get there. It may not be right away and it may not come until you least expect it.

If you 'Let It Go!,' and 'Don't Brace Yourself, Embrace Yourself,' you are ready to 'Set Sail Without an Anchor.'

We are often our own worst enemy, our harshest critic. Therefore, we sometimes serve as our own anchor. The captain of the ship rarely drops the anchor himself. He orders people to do it for him. Thus, if you want something in life or out of it, do not give a command for anyone to drop anchor, including yourself, until your destination has arrived.

Do not be afraid to slow down, pause or if you happen to veer off-course. Sh*t happens! This third step happens so much better and easier after the first two.

By all means, have a plan, a sound one at that. But do not limit yourself to what you have written down as if it were some immaculate itinerary or etched-in-stone time table.

Dr. Buxton, my therapist back in Evansville, used to tell me a pretty accurate description or diagnose of what he saw in me. 'There is nothing wrong with me or what I want in life. There is just fault in the way or ways I go about getting them.'

It is true. After limiting myself for years, I overdid the 'Set Sail without an Anchor' part and sometimes got burned out. The stress would overwhelm me, as my plate got too full to subdue the hunger or appetite I have for success and happiness.

It is ok to want something for yourself in life but you can't go crazy about it. You can't force it, you just have to deal with it head on . . . 'Set Sail . . .'

Anchors are heavy for a reason. They are not made out of plastic because of the material's durability. They are made out of metal, hard and bulky with utility and function. Thus, an anchor is just as heavy to set as it is to lift one.

This step is a little short but it is also the most straight-forward one of the four. As soon as you place an anchor down in your life, you have to exert more strength in hoisting back onto your ship, sometimes more than what you did in just getting it there. Why go through all that wasted energy, effort and strength? Save it for the 'Sail.'

4. Take Everything In and . . . Breathe

    When it rains, it pours. That is dead-on accurate in my life. For instance, I moved to Los Angeles in the May 2011. I transferred with Red Robin from Evansville, IN to Northridge, CA, starting a part-time internship with Lightning Bolt-USA, meeting five new roommates, writing this book, continuing therapy and counseling, in addition to preparing for a move to Iowa, to begin my masters.

    During all of this, I landed a wonderful and amazing position with Adidas Sports Performance on the 3rd Street Promenade in Santa Monica, CA doing visual merchandising and some selling on the sales floor.

    I held down so many jobs and hours at everything, I did not get to enjoy California as much as I wanted to. I would drive down from my apartment, which was two blocks from the campus of USC, to Hermosa Beach and run. I would lift at the Anytime Fitness there when I could.

I rarely went out to parties or the clubs. I did not participate in roadies to Anaheim for Disney or drives to San Francisco or San Diego like others did. I buried myself in working multiple jobs, writing and planning for the next move, Iowa. Who does that sh*t?

You have to 'Take Everything In . . . . And Breathe!' Before you know it, what you should be enjoying good be less, or gone. How would you know what you truly have or had if you did take time out of your day and just '. . . breathe?!'

Again, I am admitting my own faults here. I take on multiple jobs, promotions, internships, projects, philanthropy and commitments because I have a habit of saying 'yes.' That is good and all to be busy and productive, but now because you are avoiding yourself, good or bad.

I am still guilty of this dangerous cycle of schedule and committal overload. My charity, my book (one & two), planning the first tour, pursuing my Master's and working two jobs has created the same sense of overwhelming prevalence.

I always make due, but sometimes at the cost of sacrificing my sanity and health before I quit something. Do not allow yourself to get to that level.

I allowed myself for years to feel nothing but negativity in regards to being sexually molested because I never saw any positives from it. I have a book, a charity, supportive friends, family members and coworkers. I also have my health and a new found appreciation to 'Take Everything In . . . and Breathe!'

Sometimes, it is not just the successes or the perks we have to 'Take Everything In . . .' with and '. . . Breathe.' There can be a surplus of bad thoughts, or a string of bad luck and misfortune. You make the most of everything, the best of any situation.

I moved to Los Angeles having my first month's rent paid and only $300.00 cash on me by the time I pulled up to Charlie & Michael's apartment in Venice before I moved into my apartment in a couple blocks from Vermont Avenue and Exposition Boulevard in L.A.

I stressed about it, getting nervous and anxious about how is this going to work. You know what, you just got to do the damn thing!

I 'Let It Go' in 2011, or at least was well on my way in starting to. I stopped 'Bracing . . .' myself and started to '. . . Embrace . . .' myself all throughout that summer in L.A. and in Iowa. I 'Set Sail without an Anchor' in February 2012 when I landed the book deal and began working on The Shades 4 U Foundation the next month in March.

Now, with this final paragraph and a nice Skinny Girl Margarita, courtesy of one of my biggest influences, Mrs. Bethenny Frankel, I can 'Take Everything In . . . and Breathe!' So now it is your turn. Follow suit and join me as a survivor, even if it is not as a victim of CSA. We all suffer and struggle . . . and quite often, that is the beauty in life.

<<< CHAPTER TEN >>>

GRATITUDE RHYMES WITH ATTITUDE

There are a number of people over the years that have managed to support, love and be there for me despite the sh*t I went through. I only hope that I have been just as loyal to them as they have to me. I am forever grateful as I have credited my positive attitude as a result for my dying breathe to always express gratitude for even the simplest but kindest of gestures and words . . . And, for the ones that proved to be fake, I have shown you the door . . . To the left!

First and foremost, my parents. My mother and father may not have known for years my dark past or deepest skeleton until the last year or two. There is no easy way to parent through something like that, but they have always supported me emotionally, financially and more. I love them both. I do not say it enough, but now is a good time to start putting it out there more. Shout out to my brothers, Peter & Cory, and my sister Shannon and our little sex monster of a half-poodle and half-bishon, Haley.

Thank you Nana, my loving, straight-forward and humorous grandmother, as I thankfully I inherited her intelligence and practical ability to be blunt. Also, a huge thanks, love and appreciation to my Aunt Sue and cousin Ryan. You both have opened out to me the last five or so years especially and I love you even more for it.

Thank you to Dong Jim Kim, Rosemary and Jung Km and your wonderful mother. I loved being at the US Martial Arts Academy and forever will hold the memories and lessons along the way. Thank you Ken Brown, Bruce Walsh, Terry Buckley, Patrick Torreabla, Richard and Jim, Chris Starkey and your amazing children Joe and Sarah, Ashley White, Brett Williams, Paul Pelefas, Sue Magan, Angela Schuler, Dave Barlog and the rest of the people I grew up with there.

Thank you to my friends from Glen Westlake Middle School: James Logan, James Phillips, Samantha Sojka Alghrim and Josh Alghrim, Megan Smith, Lauren Kroll, Larnell Lee, Joe Feest, Brandon Street, Claire Baker, Brad Sailor, Andrea Simonetti, Jill Gottfried, Stephanie Klenotich, Ashley Hogan, Jessica Garringer, Alanna Moore, Travis Rossow, Mac Rewer, Madi Martinez, Justin Chelowa, Justin Regnier, Chalie Ammonds, Mike Dahdal, Tracy O'Connor, Judy Miller, Tim Brown, Steve Perkins and Kyle Herlache.

Thank you to Kyle Hafstad, Hilary Weston, Ashley Natonski, Joe Monahan, Ben Barron, Heather Noonan, Darrah Craig, Teena Aikara, Sarah Choi, Caroline and Emily Stewart, Allison Gibson, Theresa Slowik,

Megan Jones Basic, Ryan & Kalyn Baumgartner, Rudy Hetzer, E.J. Stockman, Dan Flaugher, Jim Gentile, Greg Rhoads, Kyle Donofrio, Brendon Osmer, Guil Noronha, Nick Dolendi, Alex DeGurian and Andrea Norton, Danielle LaVeau, Casey Cordova, Brian Kenney, Mark Vujovic, Mike Timmer, Mike Garcia, Caitlyn Miller, Lauren Cheek, Lindsey Vervoort, Kiley Tirreno, Kelly Sliwinski, Rachel Sinnen, Lisa Sickinger, Mike Stupica, Melissa Crosse, Keith and Brian Healy, Todd Samples, Joe Sumrak, Ryan Jeanes, Ryan Lazarus, Shelley Bahan, Amber Rae Lambke, Brynn Harbert, Burke Baldwin, Colleen Tabin (Cusmano), Matt Madera, Shanna St. Pierre, Megan Wheeler . . . oh and Ben Beasley.

To the best friends anyone, no matter what, could have ever had in college: Kyle Ramsy, Lani (Hadley) Cameron and her husband Nathan, April Chappelle, James Webb, Paul Best, Kyle Evans, Shawn McCormick, Brian Enders, Zach Knutsen, Melissa Ball, Lindsay Strauch, Christian Vester, Laura KW!, Jack Bryant, Amanda Betz, Melissa Deavers, Valerie Smeltzer, Janelle Swainder (I may have spelled that wrong, so sorry!), Natalie Wesley, Ayesha & Zane Forte, Annette Campbell, Roniah Walker, Courtney Brooks, James Scott, Cleo Hall, Moses Jones, Brent Lyle, Dr. Virgil and the rest of the Trendz of Essence Family. Thank you to Funmbi Elemo, Caitlin & Vince Cavallaro, Melinda X. (not taking the chance of butchering your last name but you rock, still!), Ranee Reed, Bill Caulton, Mike Shanahan, Zach Shale, Jake Ziemmer, Hilary Anderson, Katelyn Balach, Megan Spalding, Adam Currier and Marty Filagamo.

I want to thank Dierdre Hartman and Jordan Callaway, two of my Executive Board Members for The Shades 4 U Foundation and dearest friends. Thanks for your continue help, support and efforts in my work and our shared interest in our charity.

A special shout out and thanks to friendships that grew or developed during this book: James Logan, Lisa Bell, Alex Dodson, Priscilla Yeomans, Stephanie Dean West, Hilary West and one of my biggest professional and personal mentors, Tim Black.

To the greatest friends in Iowa who helped me get through my writing, transition and previous roommate drama: Austin Zabeli, Bryant Grimmius, KC Williams, Sarah Rose & Phil Wulfekuhle, Stacy Klein, Brittany Clark & Kyle Hedges, Justin Schreffler & Alex Myers, Andre Paulson, Ryan Sletten, Jesse Priest, Reece Gerleman, Nick Hinzman & Alyx Sandbothe, Sadie Range, Brian Tyne, Jesse Truax, Natalie Forsythe, Lauren Dougall, Alyssa Stevenson, Aaron Sass & Sara Durston, Cory Schmitt, Ross Droppert, Dustin Deery, Nicole Hamilton and the Staff at the Family YMCA of Black Hawk County & Life-Line Resources, as well as Hinduja Global Services.

Sonny Nguyen and Cheryl Boyd (Kate & Nick and Kim Le, too) . . . You all have been so great to me, as friends and another family. From the times I have had both pleasures of working at Metro and to playing cards and going out to eat. I love you all so much! Thank you Jeff Fossett, Zach Roesch, Shawna Henshaw, and the rest of the staff there. Coach Trent, you get a special thanks for the hook up with Lightning Bolt—USA and always being ready to supervise when I decide to 'bolt' town! I also want to thank the Holy Rosary volleyball team, girls and family, especially Mrs. Lesley & Mr. Brad Thompson and their children Ellen, Brice and Blake. Shout out to Connie & John Freeman, thanks for an awesome summer (2012) of memories and hanging out . . . here's to even more this coming summer.

I want to thank all of the people from Old Chicago. Joey Tornatore and Byron Kirk (Captain Kirk): You both have paved the way and provided me with multiple windows and opportunities to succeed. I am forever grateful for that gentleman. To David Wyatt (Danny Tanner) and Brittney Shuler (Mrs. B!), you two have pushed me forward professionally and personally, further than I thought I could during a time I needed it the most. Thank you to Natasha Ferguson, Kaylee Mowry and Joey Dumes for putting up with my crazy overwhelmed ass and being super supportive of my endeavors. You both have been a great reference and even greater friends/bosses. Michelle Romanic, I miss you at OC and I am so glad you have helped share my happiness during this time. Daniel 'Monster (Garage)' Austin . . . I give you so much credit because you have proven that one of my biggest fears of divorce is not the end all in love. You have a beautiful fiancée and an amazing set of kids from the few times I have seen them. Thank you for being a hard ass with me. Oh and yah, and why did you cheat on Sandra Bullock?! Not cool older brother. Speaking of family, what up Uncle Richard (Bennett) . . . Shout outs to Paul Sebree (my sand volleyball PIC), Megan Penninger (gosh, you look so much like Rose McGowan and talk like her . . . it's hott!), Andrea 'A.D.' Davids, Alex Wilke, Dawn Martinez, Carlos Shane, Scott Mammolenti, Matt Wilm, Rachel Hadley, Becky Peckerill, Tanya Gibson, Crystal Siscel, Laura Ames and her husband Jimmy, Debbie Turpin, Jennie Lightburne & her husband Larry, Grant Tanner, Adam Tooley & Lyndsie E., Mrs. Monya Lewis (what up, A-town . . . potential future 404-crashers lol), Sarah Whobrey & Wezley Whobrey (no relation, but you girls are like the sisters of sweetness and very incredible people), Aliy Mortimer, Susan Salters & Lisa Vanderkooy, Crystal Chambers, Kim Henry, James Oglesby, Brandon Dowdell, Zach Fegan, Matt Drone, Virginia & her soon-to-be/now husband Brian, Juan Wall, Andrew Farmer, Chole Cobb, Tiffany Kemper and Brittany Stites, as well as Israel & Joel and the rest of the staff and personnel at the restaurant . . . you all have been incredible reinforcements of what I am doing with my life and career. I love it! Also, shout out to My O.C. peeps . . . Tina and Kevin and Larisa Doyle, Fred (F-Squared) Frank, his girlfriend Kristi Wildt Owens & Jared Scales, Mr. Mike Cannon and his wife Lisa.

A huge shout-out to many of the people from some of my favorite television shows, as the entertainment and motivation to pursue my path have been very inspirational and uplifting.

Thank you to BreakSk8, the first of my America's Best Dance Crew heroes: Thank you Tony Zane (your work ethic and aspirations are unmatched dude), Jordan McQuiston, Shannon Anthony, Tyson Neal, Diamond

Walker and Jessy Nice. Fanny Pak: Matt Cady, Tiffani Grant, Meg Lawson, Glenda Morales, Cara Horibe, Phil Collins and Beau Fournier. You danced like Champs and moved your way into my life, prayers and heart. I love my new friends from the ATL, Royal Flush: Gissette Valentin, Dakota Smith (thanks for all your support even during my days in Indiana before LA. You are one talented man, good sir.), Aaron and Jared James, Cordaral Harper, Tim Conkel and Jared Mullgrav . . . You all have kept it ROYAL! Jungle Boogie and Jungle Boogie Foundation: Raqi Carter & Kenneth Tipton (I love our late night text conversations during our 'office hours' and being able to support one another's endeavors.), Antwan Thomas, Beejay Harris, Anthony & Antwain Hart (You both have such bright personalities; I love your 'Origin of Jungle Boogie' story.), Adrian Eaton & Codie Wiggins. [I shout out to you all every time with the chest pound during volleyball, or other big moments in my life.]

I have a huge amount of gratitude and admiration for celebrities such as Justin Timberlake, as Future Sex/Love Sounds quite possibly saved my life in college. You are a man of great respect and many talents. If we ever meet, I have two great stories to share (nothing creepy, scout's honor). To Andy Roddick, as you are an athlete, celebrity and great man of philanthropy. I draw inspiration to reach so many with such charisma. Channing Tatum, dude . . . you can flipping dance and romance. I got so many notes on your swag, there are notebooks upon notebooks (figurative metaphor, I do not buy that many paper products in the age of laptops and technology.).

One of the most random, but single-handed inspiring motivators to write, share, open-up and do 'W-E-R-K-!': Mrs. Bethenny Frankel. You are a strong woman who any man would be proud of to have as their wife, mother and friend. I hope our paths cross someday as well. Andy Cohen and his Real Housewives franchise. Your 'hustlers in heels' as I call them, have captured me as an audience and interest of mine that fuels my goals and ambitions, odd enough.

Though, I am not ready to announce a Faith or my Faith, for that matter, I think it is safe to say and admit that I may permit God to enter my life and dedicate my future to Him. I have never ruled it out, so perhaps the first step forward should be mine: Thank You God! I love my life, the people and projects that it holds, as I look forward to even more of both.

Thank you, the reader, for helping me be heard and giving a voice to the other victims and survivors of Child Sexual Abuse (CSA). I hope this first book is just the beginning of a meaningful and successful career of writing with a purpose. If you would like to support The Shades 4 U Foundation and help in the fight against CSA, share word of this book and encourage friends and family to go out and purchase it, as half of my intake from the book goes straight to the charity. For more information check us out on Facebook, our visit us at http://shades4ufoundation.wix.com/main.